The Manual that never came with your Child

JANE JARVIS
and DEBBIE DE JONG

Published by Struik Publishers (a division of New Holland Publishing (South Africa) (Pty) Ltd)
New Holland Publishing is a member of Avusa Ltd
Cornelis Struik House, 80 McKenzie Street, Cape Town 8001
86 Edgware Road, London, W2 2EA, United Kingdom
Unit 1, 66 Gibbes Street, Chatswood, NSW 2067, Australia
218 Lake Road, Northcote, Auckland, New Zealand

www.struik.co.za

Publishing manager: Linda de Villiers
Managing editor: Cecilia Barfield
Editor: Gavin Barfield
Designer: Helen Henn
Indexer: Barbara Ellion
Illustrator: Sandy Lightley
Photographer: Sean Calitz

Reproduction: Hirt & Carter Cape (Pty) Ltd
Printing and binding: Hengyuan Printing, China

ISBN 978-1-77007-663-1

10 9 8 7 6 5 4 3 2 1

www.imagesofafrica.co.za

IMAGES OF AFRICA
PHOTO LIBRARY

Over 40 000 unique African images available to purchase from our image bank at www.imagesofafrica.co.za

ACKNOWLEDGEMENTS

To John Taylor: You don't know us but we know you and we have learnt so much valuable information from you that we share with our clients on a daily basis. Thank you.

To all the other professionals who so willingly share their knowledge and from whom we have gained so much over the years: Thank you.

To all our clients: We have learnt as much from you as you have learnt from us. Here is the manual that so many of you have asked for. Enjoy, and we hope that it helps to consolidate all that you have already learnt.

To all at Struik who have helped to make this book a reality: Thank you for all your hard work and enthusiasm. You were our first 'readers' and we are so grateful for all your positive encouragement.

Contents

INTRODUCTION

You read pregnancy books, played Mozart, rubbed vitamin E oil on your stretch marks, and survived pregnancy and birth. You read baby books, burped your baby, learnt how to change nappies and make homemade vegetables in order to survive babyhood. You moved all your precious belongings above the one-metre mark, managed potty training and some volcanic tantrums, and survived the toddler years. But, as soon as toddlers are out of nappies, they are off to school, and just when you thought you knew it all, a whole new world of learning begins. Getting ready for school in the morning, finishing homework and getting school projects done on time are just some of the battlefield areas you may encounter with your school-going child. Not to mention studying for tests and exams and managing all the afternoon activities!

As practitioners working in the area of education and offering emotional and remedial support to both children and their parents, we have heard many battle stories. 'My child won't eat', 'My child won't listen to me', 'My child is in charge of our family' and very commonly, 'Who said having children was easy?' On numerous occasions we have also been asked, 'Why didn't this child come with a manual?' Well here it is - *The Manual that Never Came with your Child.*

What is this book all about?

Although this book is based on research, it is down to earth and practical. It covers many topics that have arisen as common problem areas during children's school years, including: organising children's bedrooms and play areas, teaching them to tidy up, morning and night time routines, being organised for extramural activities and fitting homework into busy afternoons, organisational strategies for getting homework done without a fight and planning ahead for projects and tests, studying for tests and exams, handling the TV menace, feeding children correctly and discipline. The plans and strategies described in this book are tried and tested and are working in real homes with normal children just like yours.

Who should read this book?

You — the parents! Parents who have survived the toddler and nursery school years and are then faced with the school years, might fall into the trap of thinking that it is children alone who start learning once they enter formal schooling. This is not true; parents also start on an equally steep learning curve, often without support.

When should you read this book?

If you are starting to think about either hitting your child or bashing your own head against the wall, then it is time to use this book! We understand that getting your child through school can be challenging and frustrating, especially in this day and age when the academic pressure on children is so much greater than it ever was in previous years. We have also discovered that many parents feel helpless and unsure about how to help their children through their school career as they have never had any training in education and their own school days feel like a lifetime ago. Hopefully, this book will remind you that you are not alone and give you some practical tips for the next step in your child's journey to adulthood.

How to use this book

This book may support what you are already doing with your children, but it may also open your eyes to a whole different way of managing your family. This can be intimidating and overwhelming to the point where you may want to give up before even starting. To avoid this, we suggest that you do not read the entire book and try to implement everything at once. The best way to use this book is to read Chapter 1 quite carefully because the concepts of positive discipline and behaviour modification covered in this chapter underpin almost every other chapter in the book and are important to understand. Although the rest of the chapters overlap at times, each chapter can stand alone. We hope that you will read and re-read the chapters relevant to you and find some tips that will help you to help your child overcome any obstacles he or she may encounter during his or her schooling years. (Please note that 'he', 'she' and 'they' have all been used at various times when referring to a child or children. To have included 'he/she' etc. on each occasion would be grammatically unwieldy.)

Hope and expectations

It does not mean that just because you 'get it right' in the early years, your child will be fine for the rest of his life. Or, if you 'get it wrong' that your child's life is doomed! The message of this book is that there is no such thing as perfect parenting, but that there is always room for change and growth. Parenting is a constant challenge to find the balance; the balance between when to listen and when to speak, and when to hold tight and when to let go. In our frantic world it is easy to lose our balance. So when you get the wobbles, hopefully this book will remind you about what is important and guide you towards finding your feet again.

Debbie de Jong and Jane Jarvis, August 2008

1 Catching the positive

I nag and nag, and nothing gets through.

All I ever do is shout at my poor kid. I hate myself.

A good smack on the bum will sort it all out.

I was smacked, and it never did me any harm.

Bribing children spoils them rotten.

Why do I always have to scream at you before you go and bath?

The behaviour that will be maintained is the behaviour that is fed

As much of this book is about modifying or re-adapting children's behaviour, the first chapter focuses on and explains the most effective way of making these changes in a way that is positive, painless and lasting for both you and your child. What you learn in this chapter about modifying children's behaviour will be referred to and applied in specific situations in later chapters. It is therefore important to read and understand this chapter thoroughly, as it will give you the foundation for all that follows.

Part 1:
Understanding behaviour modification

Changing behaviour the traditional way - beware of what works

Parents and teachers, in fact many adults, lament the modern taboo against spanking children as a way of disciplining them. 'Spare the rod and spoil the child,' the traditionalists rant. 'A good smack never hurt anyone, and your child will know who is boss!'

Yes – smacking children works. A good hard spanking will stop an inappropriate behaviour in its tracks. It will bring your child to a complete halt as he or she tries to assimilate how it can be that the same beloved parent who kisses them and tucks them into bed at night can turn into Stephen King's worst nightmare.

A good spanking – as well as other forms of punishment that involve threats of embarrassment, isolation, rejection, humiliation, pain or fear – will work in the short term, but may cause so much long-term damage that they should be avoided at all costs. By now you are probably saying to yourself, 'Stop! I disagree – I was punished as a child, and *I'm* OK! What's this pathetic, namby-pamby "new age" nonsense?'

The question is – are you *really* OK? *Did* you escape unscathed? Try answering these questions, and you will very soon find the answer.

- Are you terrified of making mistakes?
- Do you work hard and do your best to avoid rejection and ridicule?
- Are you anxious?
- Are you a people-pleaser, to the point of being thought a doormat?

- Do you find it hard to accept praise?
- Do you avoid authority?
- Are you fearful of people in positions of authority?
- Can you cope with conflict, or do you become aggressive or withdraw from the situation?
- Are you slightly (or very) nervous about what other people think of you?
- Do you still feel a strong need to please your parents?
- Do you feel that you are never quite good enough?

If you answered 'yes' to some of these questions (and, be assured, most people do), you are discovering that although the punishment you experienced as a child probably stopped some long-forgotten inappropriate behaviour, that punishment has nevertheless left its mark.

What is the alternative? More carrots, fewer sticks

Despite punishment being quite dangerous – and, in fact, at times abusive – many parents continue to punish their children because they simply don't know what else to do. Fortunately, there is a way to change behaviour by using a technique called behaviour modification that has beneficial rather than painful long-term effects.

1. WHAT IS BEHAVIOUR MODIFICATION?
Simply put, it's a way of changing or modifying behaviour by focusing on and rewarding positive, appropriate behaviour and, as far as possible, ignoring inappropriate behaviour.

2. WHY DOES BEHAVIOUR MODIFICATION WORK?
Behaviour modification operates on two basic underlying principles that influence human behaviour:

Principle 1: We are motivated more by praise than by punishment.
Principle 2: We work better if we are rewarded for our efforts.

Principle 1: We are motivated by praise
Behaviour modification works because it encourages people to reward what is being done well, rather than punish what is being done poorly. This focus on the positive has enormous implications both for changing behaviour and for maintaining those changes over time.

To understand this better, imagine yourself in this situation:
You have a boss who constantly points out what you haven't done. Your days at work are constant reminders of your alleged incompetence. How do you respond?

Do you feel motivated to do better?

No. You actually start to 'slack off'.

Do you have a respectful relationship with your boss?

No. You hate and despise him or her, and fantasise about hiring a hit-man.

Are you willing to follow new routines or procedures?

No. In fact you will probably sabotage them.

Are you honest with your boss?

No. You become sneaky and underhand, and do little things to 'get even' ...

Are you happy?

Absolutely not. You feel resentful, hostile, aggressive, frustrated, ignored, diminished and discouraged.

> You haven't sent the e-mail, ordered lunch, phoned the suppliers, filed the memos ...

> Lunch! How about arsenic in your sushi? – and I'll look for another job while you die a slow death!

Now imagine the opposite situation. You have a great boss. He or she notices what you do well and responds to your successes. He or she says 'thank you', 'please' and 'well done'. Your efforts are acknowledged and your mishaps are dealt with privately and considerately. *Now* how do you respond?

Do you feel motivated to do better?

Always. Achievements are recognised, so the effort is worth it.

Do you have a respectful relationship with your boss?

Very much so.

Are you willing to follow new routines or procedures?

Absolutely. You will probably do almost anything your boss asks, because it makes you both feel good.

Are you honest with your boss?

Completely.

Are you happy?

Very. You feel satisfied, encouraged, special, acknowledged, rewarded, included and fulfilled.

Now let's apply these situations to your relationship with your child. Within your family, you are the boss. What type of boss are you? One who consistently and sharply focuses on the negative, or one who focuses on the positive, and rewards it? Is there a strand of negativity that characterises the relationships amongst your family members, or do you take pleasure in each other's successes? The type of 'boss' you choose to be in your family will directly affect the way your children behave. If your children are difficult, look to your leadership style before you blame 'the little terrors'!

Principle 2: We are more motivated to work for rewards

Even if you love your job and feel emotionally satisfied and happy in your workplace, the chances of your working without payment are probably nil. As adults we all work for rewards, which are usually financial.

If, as adults, we need to be coaxed along with rewards, why is it that we always seem to expect children to work for nothing? Children are also motivated by reward; probably more so than adults – so it makes sense to use rewards when trying to change their behaviour.

Not only does the use of rewards work in tandem with one of the fundamental principles that influence human behaviour, it also corresponds with children's first stage of moral development (i.e. that children act to get a reward or to avoid a negative consequence).

Behaviour modification and the stages of moral development

If you understand the stages of moral development, you will understand why rewards work for children and why rewards are not the same thing as bribery and corruption.

Psychologist Lawrence Kohlberg described seven stages of moral development which have contributed enormously to our understanding of human behaviour and discipline. Here are the stages at a glance:

Level	Stage	Motivation for behaviour
Pre-conventional level (ages 4–10)	Stage 1	Act to avoid negative consequences
	Stage 2	Act to receive reward
Conventional level (ages 10–13)	Stage 3	Act to avoid disapproval of others
	Stage 4	Act in accordance with law and duty
Post-conventional level (ages 13–adulthood)	Stage 5	Act to maintain respect of others
	Stage 6	Act to uphold one's own principles
	Stage 7	Act in accordance with universal principles

- **STAGES 1 AND 2**

The first two stages of moral development occur at the pre-conventional level of development. These are the stages of survival. The main behavioural motivation at this level is obedience – either as a way of avoiding negative consequences, or to earn a reward.

Although stages 1 and 2 are the first stages in a child's moral development, they don't, in fact, have much to do with morals. During these stages, children are externally motivated, either by the threat of punishment or the prospect of a reward. You cannot, at this stage, ask a child to do something because it is 'the right thing to do', because this concept is simply beyond their moral understanding.

Conversations like these simply do not work as a way of disciplining young children or changing their behaviour. This is not because they are little brats or horrible children, but because, at this developmental level, they do not have the capacity to look outwards with compassion. Children at this level are highly egocentric, and their behaviour is ruled by 'What's in it for me?' So, when you ask your four-year-old to share his toys with his friend and he throws a tantrum, you know why! This level of moral development usually ends at around age ten, but this is not set in stone. Some children move into the next phase of moral development, which involves acting to receive the approval of others or to avoid disapproval, at ages earlier than ten – and some people *never* move out of this phase of moral development. There are many adults who will not do something for others unless there is something in it for them.

- **STAGES 3 AND 4**

Stages 3 and 4 occur at the conventional level of moral development. During these stages there is a shift in the factors that drive behaviour. In stage 3 we are motivated to behave appropriately to avoid disapproval (as opposed to punishment), and in stage 4 we start to do things because what we are doing is honourable and what the rules dictate. This is why your child shouts at you if you don't stop at a stop-street, or if you cross the road in the wrong place. You are breaking the rules.

- **STAGES 5, 6 AND 7**

The final three stages of moral development involve the post-conventional level of morality. All actions and behaviours are driven by reason rather than emotions and feelings. As has been mentioned previously, many individuals never reach these stages of development.

Based on these levels of moral development, it becomes clear that using rewards makes sense, because they work with and complement children's moral development. This is why the use of rewards works so well, and why it is strongly recommended as part of a discipline system. It is also important to note that no matter what a child's age, if you want to change their behaviour, drop back to the first levels of moral development and offer the child an incentive to be co-operative. If the incentive suits the child's age and is something that they really want, their behaviour should change for the better.

Part 2:
How to use behaviour modification

You now know that behaviour modification relies on focusing on and rewarding appropriate behaviour, but understanding *why* it works is the easy part. In part 2, we learn how to use this discipline technique effectively.

In order to learn how to use behaviour modification, we will examine a scenario that is familiar to thousands of parents. Your child is driving you insane! Every morning brings the same battle – getting dressed. Your child fiddles and dawdles and makes the whole family late. What can you do?

Exploring familiar, traditional discipline strategies

If I've asked you once, I've asked you a thousand times – go and get dressed!

STRATEGY 1: YOU NAG

Does this work? No!

These days, children are not particularly good at responding to information that they hear. Your voice, especially if you nag repeatedly, simply fades out of your child's field of focus. A nagging voice (like the whining of a mosquito) is boring, repetitive, irritating and something to be ignored.

STRATEGY 2: YOU SCREAM (ALSO A TYPE OF NAG, BUT LOUDER)

Does this work? No!

Shrieking at your child will probably have the desired effect, but by the time you start shouting and screaming you are probably at the end of your tether. You feel dreadful, you look like a mile of bad road, you are exhausted, and your child goes off to school muttering and mumbling about how horrible and mean you are.

STRATEGY 3: YOU THREATEN AND PUNISH

Does this work? No!

Threats and punishment do not work because inevitably, in the heat of the moment, when you are red in the face and panting with rage, you end up saying something completely irrational.

Although some threats and forms of punishment *do* work, they usually involve taking something valuable away from your child. Parents often take away television privileges, dock pocket money, or go to the extreme of denying a child a favourite sport or banning them from seeing friends. As we saw earlier in this chapter, while this will probably improve your child's behaviour, it will also affect your relationship and could well set the stage for aggression, defiance, revenge or withdrawal, which could surface during adolescence. How often have you heard the parents of adolescents say, 'But what have we done? Where did we go wrong?'

STRATEGY 4: YOU IGNORE

Does this work? No!

Young children are egocentric, and they want to be the centre of attention at all times. Ignoring them completely will precipitate *any* action at all that gets your attention back. Frequently, because we are quicker to punish than praise, a child will do something really, really naughty because this will get you to respond very quickly. It does not matter that your response is punitive, angry, or even dangerous. Children would rather have negative attention than no attention at all.

STRATEGY 5: YOU SMACK OR HURT PHYSICALLY

Does this work? Don't even go there!

Later in the conversation ...

If these traditional strategies worked, we would live in a world of perfectly behaved children. Clearly, this is not the case. We need another option – and behaviour modification fits the bill.

Exploring behaviour modification one step at a time

STEP 1: TARGETING THE INAPPROPRIATE BEHAVIOUR

Your first step when using behaviour modification is to choose *one* behaviour that you want to change. Discuss with your child what it's going to be.

When you choose a behaviour to modify, *be specific*. For example, 'brushing your teeth after breakfast without having to be reminded' is specific; while 'being good' is too vague, because what you think is being good and what your child thinks is being good are often two different things. 'Getting ready for school in time' is too complicated, since it involves too many steps. If you do everything else, but forget to put your lunch tin in your bag, for example, you don't get a reward.

A rule of thumb is to reward an appropriate action; something that your child does. Rewarding behavioural attitudes – for example, rewarding 'sharing', 'kindness' or 'fairness' is tricky, because it is subjective. Your and your child's opinion of what constitutes kindness may be rather different.

Rather try to attach an action to the behaviour, for example: 'You can show kindness and consideration by taking your plate to the sink after dinner.'

STEP 2: NEGOTIATING THE REWARDS

You can't decide what the reward is to be without your child's input, because the reward must be something that your child values highly. Rewards must, however, not be ridiculously expensive or extravagant.

Little rewards that work well are:

- Money (small amounts at a time).
- Cell phone airtime (a few additional minutes at a time).
- Lunchbox treats.
- Extra tuck money.
- Extra television/PlayStation time.
- A longer bedtime story, or even an extra story.
- More time with a parent/significant adult. You may be surprised to learn that the most effective rewards, and the ones that children most often ask for, involve spending one-on-one quality time with an adult whom they love. So, the promise of an extra-long bedtime story, some soccer, or even playing a computer game together can be very effective.

STEP 3: LINK PRAISE TO THE REWARDS

Every time your child behaves appropriately, make sure the child not only gets the rewards, but praise as well. You may not believe this, but children love making their parents happy and proud. So, when you praise an appropriate behaviour and show your happiness, pride and thanks, the behaviour is very likely to be repeated.

In fact, some children may start to value the praise they receive more than the tangible reward, because it makes them feel good and enhances their self-esteem. By praising your children at the same time as giving a reward, you help to shift them to a higher level of moral development.

To be effective, praise must be:

- Genuine, and not gushy. A simple 'thank you' will do.

- Timely and consistent.

Praise as soon as the behaviour occurs and, to begin with, every time the behaviour occurs. Inconsistency ruins the effectiveness of this discipline technique.

- Specific to the behaviour.

Praise and reward the behaviour specifically. For example, say 'thank you for taking your plate to the sink', rather than 'thank you for being good'. Remember, you are targeting a specific behaviour, so all praise and rewards must be linked to that behaviour.

STEP 4: REWARDING THE ACTION

Rewards are to be given if, and *only* if, your child has behaved appropriately. If the rule is that your child will get a reward if she or he gets dressed in ten minutes, then stick to this. Eleven minutes is too slow and, even though close, it is not what you agreed on – therefore no reward, and no arguments. Stay firm.

How to reward children

People are often uneasy about rewarding children because they believe that once they start, the children will always expect a reward for doing something good. This is not true if rewards are given properly and, in fact, you can teach your children some valuable lessons in life by rewarding them. This is how you do it:

1ST STAGE: INSTANT REWARDS

To begin with, during the first week (maybe longer with younger children), you have to reward and praise the desired new behaviour every time it occurs. By endowing the new behaviour with as much praise, reward and encouragement as possible, you will ensure that the behaviour is repeated, because your child will strive to earn your positive attention and the treat that goes with it. During this stage you are trying to establish a link in your child's mind that it pays to be good.

2ND STAGE: DELAYED GRATIFICATION

During the next week you can start to delay the rewards, but not the praise. If the reward for getting dressed in ten minutes is R2, then you can praise the behaviour and tell your child that they have earned their money, but that you will save all the money they earn this week and that they can have it on Friday. This is better, as the child will learn that you can't do much with a small reward like R2, for example. But if you have R10 on Friday, you can buy so much more. In this way your child will learn to delay gratification, and to reap the rewards of waiting. This is an important life lesson – many adults end up in therapy because they have never learned to delay gratification, and end up getting themselves into all sorts of trouble.

3RD STAGE: INTERMITTENT REWARDS

By the third week you can start to reward intermittently, but you must still praise often. By rewarding intermittently your child never knows when it is worthwhile to behave, so he or she will make sure they behave well, just in case today is the day when a reward might be earned.

This stage is important. If you reward consistently for too long, the treat becomes a habit, and is no longer as appealing. Also, you do not want your child to behave appropriately only if there is a tangible reward. It is in stage 3 that you start to shift your child's moral development from a pre-conventional level to a conventional level (See Kohlberg's levels of moral development in Part 1); from behaving well to earn a reward to behaving well because they want to please you and follow the rules. By offering intermitent rewards you also teach your child another life lesson – that sometimes in life you have to do things and you get nothing back for it!

4TH STAGE: STOPPING ONE AND STARTING ANOTHER

After about three weeks to a month, you will probably find that you no longer need rewards; nor do you have to praise continually. Your child's behaviour will have changed and become a habit. This is when you start to work on the *next* behaviour you have chosen. But it is important to note that if you never again comment on the good behaviour that has just been targeted, after a couple of weeks your child may slip back into his or her old ways. So remember every now and again to notice the behaviour and to thank your child for their continued co-operation, or to reward them every now and again for maintaining their good behaviour. In this way they will continue to behave well, because somebody notices and appreciates it.

Using star charts

Star charts work in much the same way as rewards, and in fact *include* rewards. The difference is the type of behaviour targeted. While using the 'instant reward, delayed gratification and intermittent rewards procedure' is good for behaviours that can be timed and which need to be speeded up, star charts are aimed at behaviours that *cannot* be timed. Examples of behaviours that can be put onto a star chart include sitting down to do homework without fussing and arguing; brushing teeth without being reminded; putting clothes in the wash basket; hanging up towels after bathing and so forth.

A star chart is designed to be used over a period of approximately three weeks; the time, according to behavioural experts, it takes to establish a habit.

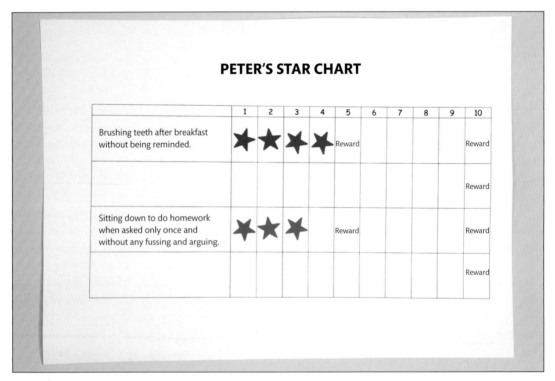

A star chart in use

HOW TO USE A STAR CHART

Step 1

Decide which behaviour is to be targeted. It is a good idea to practise using star charts with *only one targeted behaviour* at first. Once you are good at star charts and consistently remember to give your child stars, you could target two behaviours at the same time. *Don't* do any more, otherwise you will find yourself saying, 'If you don't do that, you won't get a star' all day, and your child will think, 'Stars, stars, stars ... all I ever hear about are these stupid old stars!'

Step 2

Negotiate the rewards up front. Children need to receive a small reward after five stars, a slightly bigger reward after ten stars, and their proper reward once they reach 20 stars. If you do not negotiate and agree on the rewards up front, you may have problems when your child doesn't like what you give them.

Step 3

Draw up the star chart and stick it up on the wall. Many parents don't actually get to this step. They tell their children that they are going to make a star chart, and even negotiate the rewards, but then forget to actually make one and instead try to keep a mental track of the stars. However, after a while everyone forgets how many stars have been obtained, arguments follow and the star chart is abandoned. Children benefit from having a visible record of their stars. Older children may not like them to be visible to everyone, but it is still important to keep a record of how many times they have met the targeted behaviour, even if this is done in a little notebook. This way there can be no arguments about when to give them their rewards.

It is better to use a numbered star chart (see example) rather than one that runs according to the days of the week. If you use a numbered system, you can start on any day of the week. Also, if a child misses a day (i.e. doesn't meet the conditions needed to get a star), there are no gaps on their chart. When they get it right the next day, they simply carry on from where they were, and it takes a day longer to reach the reward.

Step 4

Every time your child behaves appropriately, stick a star on the chart – but remember that a child only gets a star if they meet the criteria completely. If you give in and give your child a star because they *almost* got the behaviour right, they learn that they don't really have to behave appropriately. You also create the potential for arguments. For example, if you have said that your child can have a star for brushing his or her teeth after breakfast without being reminded and you start to ask, 'Have you brushed ...' but your child quickly tells you before you finish your sentence that they are on their way to the bathroom, it amounts to a reminder and no star can be given. If you do give your child a star, tomorrow you will find them in the TV room and, when you ask whether they brushed their teeth, there will be a long story about 'I was just coming past this room to get something, but I'm on my way to the bathroom.' Of course they will also ask for a star and, when you say no, they will say, 'But yesterday you gave me a star ...' and an argument will follow. Then you may as well scrunch up the star chart and throw it away.

Don't be scared not to give stars in case your child cries. Tears are good. They are very therapeutic. But if your child is cross with you, label their feelings for them. Say something like: 'You think you are cross with me for not giving you a star, but actually you are disappointed with yourself for not getting the star. Don't worry about it, though ... try again tomorrow and you will get a star, and you will still get your reward – it'll just take one day longer, that's all.' If your child cannot accept this and is out of control, send them to their room for a while or walk away and give them no attention. This is called 'time out'. (Time Out is discussed in detail later in the book. It is a very useful disciplinary technique to know about.)

Handy hints

✎   A lapse in behaviour is not the end of the world; it is natural. Don't let a lapse lead you back into using unsuccessful strategies. No behaviour change occurs perfectly overnight (you will know this if you have ever tried to stop smoking or to stick to a new diet).

✎   Never take stars or rewards away. This is punishment, and goes completely against the principles of behaviour modification. (Imagine if you made a mistake at work and your boss docked your salary – you would be furious!) If your child has earned that R10, don't subtract any money if she or he lapses. Rather dismiss the lapse with as little fuss as possible. Behaviours that do not get much reaction are not worthwhile repeating. Remember that children love attention, especially their parents' attention.

✎   Behaviour modification only works when changing one – or possibly two – behaviours at a time. Don't expect to be able to use behaviour modification to 'fix' every one of your child's bad habits in one go. You will both lose your minds in the attempt!

✎   If you are still a firm believer in punishment and think that behaviour modification is for sissies, then don't even start. You have to believe in the underlying principles of behaviour modification, otherwise you will try it half-heartedly, and it won't work for you.

✎   Adults in the home must demonstrate a united front. It is impossible for only one parent to use this strategy.

✎   If your child is spoiled and gets treats often and for no particular reason (for example, granny brings a present every time she visits; you buy toys or some other kind of treat every time you go shopping, or you give in to demands because you are terrified of tantrums), then behaviour modification will be a difficult, but not impossible, adjustment. You first need to stop all these treats and to tell your child that in future they will have to earn them. Then you actually have to stop buying the treats!

✎   Using behaviour modification is not difficult, but it is not a quick-fix solution. It can be a slow and painstaking process that can really try your patience. The benefits, however, last a lifetime – so it is worth putting in the initial effort. Later in the book there are further examples of how to use the technique effectively if you are still feeling a little overwhelmed or unsure of how to implement the process (particularly in Chapter 3).

2 Organising the bedroom

> Honestly, if I don't do it, it will never get done!

> He's so untidy and disorganised. He would forget his head if it wasn't attached to his body!

> He always leaves things at home, and I have to rush to school to drop them off for him.

> Her room is a pigsty. I'm sure there are things growing under the bed!

> She loses her stuff all the time. I've bought three jerseys this year already!

A place for everything, and everything in its place

Planning and organisation are not skills that occur naturally. They have to be taught. Many adults make the mistake of expecting children simply to be organised; to be able to tidy their room and pack their school bag as a matter of course. This expectation of children's capabilities is where all the careful planning and organisation can become a minefield!

Planning and organisation:
What does this really mean?

Planning simply means the steps that an individual takes in order to solve problems or to reach goals.

These planning steps are:

DETERMINING

This means being aware that there is a problem to solve, and understanding the nature of the problem. It may also simply involve deciding on a goal.

SELECTING AND ORGANISING

This means deciding what actions to take, and in what order to perform the actions to solve the problem or reach the goal.

APPLICATION

This means taking action.

EVALUATION

This means deciding if the application or action is working, and whether to continue with or abandon it.

Where do planning and organisation occur in the brain?

Being able to plan and 'get organised' is often really difficult and can cause a lot of tension in the home. Many children struggle to develop plans and use them to stay organised. Before explaining how to help your child learn these skills, some background on the areas in the brain where planning and organisation occur is needed.

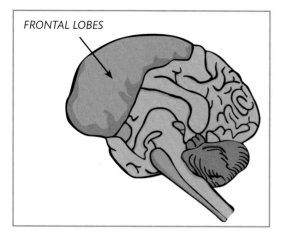

FRONTAL LOBES

Planning and organisation are part of the 'executive functioning' repertoire of the brain. This means that, just as at the executive level of a corporation, management and critical decisions are made in the frontal lobes.

As important as they are, the frontal lobes are the last part of the brain to develop, and only do so from about four to five years of age. This is why you cannot reason with a very young child.

Left: The frontal lobes are important for planning and organisation, reasoning, logic and deduction

A statement like this or any other form of reasoning probably won't work with young children

Getting to the nitty-gritty!

Keeping the bedroom and/or playroom organised and tidy

Being organised is not the same as being neat and tidy. It means being able to find things easily in the least amount of time; something essential for keeping the wheels of family life moving along smoothly.

STEP 1: CUT OUT CLUTTER

The more clutter there is in a bedroom or playroom, the more difficult it will be for your child to keep it tidy and well organised. So, your first step is to sort out the toys, stationery and clothes in your child's room. You can make three piles:

Pile A: Clutter to throw out or donate. This pile includes broken toys, outgrown toys, clothes that don't fit or are never worn, and any other bits and pieces that take up space but have no use. HINT: Be ruthless, and don't do this when your child is around or nothing will leave the room! If you are uncertain about anything, keep it aside and check with your child first.

Pile B: This pile is for toys, clothes and other bits and pieces that are no longer suitable for your child, but have high sentimental value or are of a high quality, like wooden toys. Pack these away for posterity. One day when you are a grandparent, you can give them to your grandchildren.

Pile C: This pile includes everything that is still suitable for your child and which is used regularly. You may find that this pile is still very big and hard to organise, as many children today have too many toys. One way to get around this is to rotate toys. Pack away the toys that your child does not play with regularly and bring them out during rainy days or school holidays, and they will seem like new toys all over again.

By rotating toys you will have a much smaller pile to sort, and fewer toys for your child to tidy up at the end of the day.

STEP 2: BOX IT!

Many of us have big, beautiful toy boxes for our children. The problem with toy boxes is that everything gets thrown into them and all they do is hide the chaos. The big toys stay on top and the little toys filter to the bottom. So, when your child searches for a small toy, the whole box has to be emptied, which means that the whole box has to be tidied. To try and avoid this, get rid of the single big box and do yourself a favour by getting hold of several smaller containers.

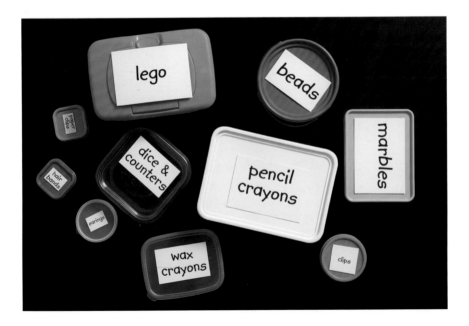

These containers are what you will use to categorise and sort the clutter.

STEP 3: SETTING UP THE STRUCTURE

As a parent, it is your job to set up the initial organisation in your child's bedroom.

Do this by creating and labelling a place for everything, and then putting everything in its place. Your child can be involved in this process, but you must create the structure.

Labels can be created in any of the following ways:

1. Written 2. Drawn either by yourself or by your child 3. Use the label from the packaging 4. Use a picture and a written label which will help your child start to recognise and read some familiar words

The containers can be used to sort and categorise smaller items like:

- Stationery (pencils in one tub, wax crayons in another and felt-tipped Kokis in another).
- Hair accessories (school clips in one tub, weekend clips in another and elastic bands in another).
- Marbles.
- Dice and game counters, etc.

The process of setting up the initial organisational structure can take some time, especially if your child has lots of things that have never been organised before. If you try to do this in a day, you will feel overwhelmed and will probably give up.

So, organise yourself before you start to organise your child. Break the process of sorting out the bedroom into do-able portions and write these down on a 'To Do' list. Here are some guidelines:

To do list:	tick
1. Clothes in drawers (e.g. underwear, school socks, sports socks, civvies socks, vests , swimming costumes, etc)	
2. Hanging clothes (e.g. school shirts, trousers, skirts, dresses, jackets, etc)	
3. Big toys (e.g. dolls, trucks, stuffed toys, puzzles and games, etc)	
4. Little toys (e.g. Lego, promotional toys, dolls clothes and accessories, marbles, small cars, etc)	
5. Stationery	
6. Sporting equipment	

STEP 4: LET YOUR CHILDREN PLAY

Once you have organised the room, you will find that your child will spend hours playing, because the toys are easy to find. They may even discover some things they had forgotten about. Don't make the mistake of making your child play with only one toy at a time and packing away this toy before the child is allowed to play with the next one. This is not how play happens, and it will stifle your child's creativity. You will end up with a room full of toys, but your child won't play with any of them, because it is too difficult.

STEP 5: MAINTAINING THE STRUCTURE

Just because you have spent hours organising your child's room does not mean that your child will automatically be able to maintain the order.

Now comes the hard part – teaching your child how to keep the room organised and tidy. Remember, it takes three weeks to form a habit. This means that you have to be involved with teaching and helping your child to stay organised for three weeks, until the 'tidy' habit is firmly in place.

This may seem like a long time now, but a three-week investment in the construction of a positive, life-long habit is one of the best gifts you will ever give to your child.

The procedure for maintaining a well-organised bedroom is as follows:

A. Do *not* shout at your child for messing up your hard work. Smile and say (even if through gritted teeth) 'Wow, it looks like you had lots of fun playing today. Let's pack all your toys away now, so that you can have fun playing again tomorrow.'

B. Do *not* pack everything away yourself while your child watches you. In no time at all they will wander off to do something more interesting and leave you to do all the work. This misses the point of the whole exercise.

C. Do not stand in your child's room and issue verbal instructions, as this will lead to your child becoming dependent on you always being around to give the commands. Rather start by telling your child that you are going to help him or her learn how to keep their room beautiful and tidy. Explain that everything in their room has a place, and that their job at the end of every day is to put all their things back into their specific places. The way to help your child learn how to do this efficiently is to allow them to create their own tidying-up routine. Ask your child what he or she thinks should be packed away first. Once they have done this, ask what they think they would like to pack away next, and so on. If you allow your child to make these decisions, the tidying-up routine will happen in a way that makes sense to your child, and won't seem like a plan imposed by you that may not feel natural to your child.

D. You now have this conversation every day for a week or two (or even three), until you see that your child has started to learn the structure and is not relying on you to tell them where things go. You must be in the room, asking the questions ('What's next?' 'What's next?'), establishing the tidy-up routine and being there to guide and support your child, but remembering to always let your child drive the process.

E. After a week or so, you can start to withdraw slightly (you may have to spend longer with younger children, but the time will be worthwhile in the end). Go into the room and start the process off. Ask the question,

'What are you going to pack away first, and what will you pack away after that?' By now your child knows exactly how to start and while he or she is busy packing, you can step out of the room for (literally) a couple of minutes. Return to the room, praise your child for what he or she has done and ask what will be packed away next. Again, once your child gets busy packing, you can leave the room for a short time.

F. As the weeks pass, your time spent out of the room can become longer and, after a while (sometimes as little as three weeks, but depending on each individual child and their age), your child should be able to tidy the room on his or her own.

Remember – it takes three weeks to develop a habit, so a child needs to see everything in the same place for at least three weeks in order to learn the system. Many parents spend time organising their children's room, but on the first day things go back in the wrong place, so the child never learns the system. The parents then have to re-organise the room in a month or two's time. This is a huge task and not always fun, so do it once properly, and then take the time to teach your children how to maintain the structure. An organised child who can find all his or her things is usually a happy child, and happy children make happy parents.

Some handy hints

✍ Never pull out of the initial start-up phase of tidying up. Always give explicit instructions and make this face-to-face. Don't yell 'tidying-up time!' from another room, because you can be sure that when you check on your child 20 minutes later, he or she will still be playing. Make sure that the child hears the instruction, stops playing and starts to tidy up before you walk away. This will save you valuable time later on.

✍ Give your child a time-related warning that they will soon have to stop playing. Don't make the mistake of saying that they have five minutes before tidying-up time, and then leave them for 20 minutes. This will interfere with their development of a sense of time and time management. If you say five minutes and leave them for longer than intended, admit the mistake and say, 'I said five minutes until tidying-up time, but you have had 17 minutes. That is 12 minutes longer than I said you could have.' In this way they will learn that five minutes is a short period of time, and 17 minutes is much longer.

✍ The 'I'm not sure' or 'I'm in a rush' box! Have an additional container in case your child or anyone unfamiliar with your system (such as visitors or your domestic worker) does not know where a specific toy goes. Encourage them to put it in this container rather than throwing it randomly into a drawer if you are not around. This container then needs to be emptied during the next tidy-up time in order to prevent it becoming the next big, chaotic toy box. Instead of putting these toys away yourself, teach your child where they go and let him or her actually put them away to reinforce the categorisation system.

3 The morning and evening routine

> Hurry up, you'll be late for school!

> For the twentieth time, go and brush your teeth!

> Mom, where are my takkies?

> If you don't hurry up we are going to leave without you!

> Why must I nag you all the time?

How to get little ones up and off – or down and out

Getting your child up and out of the door in time for school, or bathed, fed and settled for bed can be as bloody a battlefield as keeping the little ones' room tidy. Fortunately, there are simple and effective ways to bring order to the morning chaos and that equally terrible time between 5pm and 7pm, often called 'suicide hour'!

Before we begin - beware the power struggle

Forewarned is forearmed

Setting up and maintaining morning and evening routines takes time and patience. Inevitably, as you try and put these structures into place, your children will test them to see how serious you are, and there is a good chance that before you get your system up and running, you and your offspring will have come head-to-head in a series of power struggles.

The first rule of power struggles is that you should avoid them at all costs – because you will never win. There is nothing as tenacious, determined and immovable as a five-year-old, or any child for that matter, who has decided not to bath.

Tips for avoiding power struggles

1. STAY CONSISTENT AND PREDICTABLE. Don't change the routine from one day to the next. This will confuse your children and they will not be able to learn the routine and stick to it. The chances are that they will become even more disorganised and difficult because they feel confused. Being inconsistent also gives children an opportunity to challenge or argue with you. For example: 'But yesterday we didn't bath before supper, so why do we have to today?'

It is also important that, if you are a two-parent family, both parents operate as a united force. The minute one parent changes the routine, the entire process will collapse and, even worse, a power struggle may develop between the parents. Establishing and maintaining an effective routine is based on whole-family buy-in. If one family member, particularly an adult, does not want to participate, it becomes a virtually impossible process.

2. FIVE MINUTES IS FIVE MINUTES. Never make the mistake of telling your children that they have five minutes to do something, and then leaving them for much longer. They will soon learn that you don't mean what you say, which gives them a perfect opportunity to duck out of a set routine – and all your efforts (and possibly your mental health) will collapse.

Not sticking to the stated time also affects children's development of a sense of time. Parents often complain that their children have no sense of time, and we have to ask whose fault this is. Parents confuse children by not sticking to stated times. For example, we tell children that there are ten minutes left until bedtime, and then get busy with our own chores and only come back half an hour later to put them to bed. The next evening we might tell them again that they have ten minutes until bedtime, but, because they are whining and we are tired, we put them to bed after just five minutes. Later, when we tell the children that it should only take ten minutes to get dressed in the morning, they think, 'The *long* ten minutes or the *short* ten minutes?'

If you give a child a time limit, and for some reason exceed that time limit (as often happens in reality), then tell your child when you come back that you said they had ten more minutes to bed, but that they have now had 23 minutes. In this way they will learn that ten minutes is a short period of time, whereas 23 minutes is much longer.

3. USE COUNTDOWNS TO PREPARE CHILDREN FOR A CHANGE IN ACTIVITY. For example if they are watching television and bath time is approaching, count them down to bath time. Do this by saying, 'It's five minutes to bath time ... two minutes to bath time ... it's bath time now; off you go.' Using a countdown usually works because, as you give the first time signal, your child's brain starts to disengage from one activity and prepare for the next. By the final time signal they have had time to disengage completely, and you will have less difficulty moving them on from one activity to the next. Quite often children become completely immersed in an activity, and if you interrupt them and bellow, 'Go and bath now!' you shatter their peace of mind because it disengages too quickly, and your child will inevitably respond by fighting with you or getting into a power struggle. If you find yourself in a power struggle even after you have given your child a countdown, always remember to offer the 'either/or' alternatives discussed in detail in the next section.

It is important to remember that when doing a countdown it is essential to keep to the stated time. Remember, five minutes is five minutes.

4. USING THE EITHER/OR APPROACH. Children, like adults, do not enjoy being told what to do, and tend to be far more co-operative when given a choice. This means that ordering your child about will get you nothing but a headache, a sore throat and a child who takes on the unappealing characteristics of a mule. Instead of the 'nag, nag, threaten and nag' approach to getting things done, rather use the 'either/or' approach. This is a powerful therapeutic technique which is sometimes used to modify the behaviour of children with oppositional defiant disorder. If it works for them, it will work for you.

Using the 'either/or' approach means giving children a choice, which immediately makes them feel as though they have some autonomy and control over their situation.

For example, if your child does not want to bath, even after the countdown, do not enter into a power struggle and start shouting. Rather counter the situation by saying something like, 'Either you bath now, or you won't get tuck money tomorrow.' The trick with this technique is to make the 'or' choice as awful as possible. For most children, bathing is the lesser evil, and they should co-operate. There is a strong chance that when starting off with the 'either/or' approach, your child will challenge you to see how serious you are. If you give your child the choice whether to bath or to lose tuck money, and he or she still refuses to bath, then they must not get their money. Remember – stay consistent, predictable, and follow through on what you say.

To this end, when using the 'either/or' approach, the 'or' must be practical and do-able. Do not make empty threats that you can't follow through. You will look silly, and your child will be quietly laughing at you. For example, do not say, 'If you do not go and bath now, you will not go to David's birthday party,' or 'If you do not go and bath now we will not go on holiday.' Of course you are going to send your child to the birthday party. You have probably bought the present already, and you know that it is bad manners not to arrive at some event that you have already said yes to. As far as the holiday is concerned, you probably need the holiday more than your child – and why would you punish yourself?

To summarise so far – planning, implementing and maintaining morning and evening routines relies on consistency, predictability, honest timekeeping, countdowns and rational choices. With this in mind, here are the steps for the morning and evening routines:

The morning routine

Many parents feel certain that they have an effective morning routine simply because they manage to eject their children, fed, clothed, washed and packed, from the house in time to get to school. When asked how they achieve this, the inevitable answer is, 'We nag, follow, threaten, cajole, bribe and even do everything for them.'

An effective morning routine does not mean following your child around like Big Brother, supervising every step of the routine. This is tiring and boring, and how are you supposed to get ready yourself? An effective morning routine is one where, after some guidance and supervision, children start to manage things on their own so that they are able to prepare for the day independently and punctually without the constant prompting of your nagging voice.

STEP 1: DO AS MUCH AS POSSIBLE THE NIGHT BEFORE

The best advice for establishing a smooth morning routine is to get as much as possible done the night before. If you and your children are packed and organised for the following day, you will avoid anxiety, sleepless nights and that dreadful, cold-sweat-inducing, chilling 3am realisation that you have forgotten to do something vital. If you all have a stress-free sleep you will have happier, calmer children in the morning and you will have pre-empted any nasty surprises, like finding out that your precious offspring have no clean socks or have left their school shoes somewhere at school.

STEP 2: A PICTURE SAYS A THOUSAND WORDS

Most parents will have noticed that their children become conveniently deaf at the sound of their voice, particularly when that voice is giving an instruction. The deafness becomes profound when that instruction is given in the morning, when you are all in a rush to get to school. Instead of giving instructions to your children, use photographs to establish their morning routine. This involves spending a morning following them about with a camera and taking photographs of them as they perform each morning activity. Capture them getting out of bed, getting dressed, eating breakfast, taking their vitamins, brushing their teeth, washing their face, putting their lunch tins in their bags, and anything else that you require them to do in the mornings. Print out a set of these photos and place them in a strategic place in your child's bedroom where he or she will see them frequently (on the outside of their cupboard door, for example). You can also print a second set of these photos and place them in the kitchen, as many families spend lots of time in their kitchens. In this way, when your child comes through to the kitchen they will continue to be reminded of what to do next. The fridge is a very good place to put the photos, as your child will see them every time he or she opens the fridge.

The sequence of routine morning activities differs from family to family. Some children brush teeth after breakfast, others brush as soon as they get up. Some families eat breakfast before getting dressed. There is no correct order, but there must be an order.

Be careful not to break up the photographs. For example do not put the 'get dressed' photo in the bedroom and the 'brush teeth' one in the bathroom. Your child is sure to get lost between the bedroom and bathroom and land up in the lounge watching cartoons. The photographs must always be together, always in the same order, and don't forget to place them at your child's eye level, either from top-to-bottom or left-to-right.

*1. Get dressed 2. Eat breakfast 3. Take vitamins 4. Brush teeth 5. Comb hair
6. Put on suncream 7. Put lunch tin in schoolbag*

WHY USE PHOTOGRAPHS?

1. By using photographs, you provide your child with a visual map or plan of the morning routine, which is easy to follow and will always stay the same. Remember, children like consistency and predictability.

2. Using photographs of your child and not generic pictures of each activity is a very powerful way of capturing their attention. Developmentally, children are very egotistical and will be drawn back repeatedly to look at photographs of themselves. In this way, they will form a strong visual imprint of the order of the morning routine through looking at the pictures; a sequence which becomes like a mini-movie. This movie will still be running in their head when they are 25, living on their own, and having to get up and get ready for work in the morning.

3. Photographs also tie in with our highly visual age, where children are better primed to respond to what they see, rather than what they hear. This is largely thanks to the invention of television. Because children today are better visual learners, photographs work better than a relentlessly nagging voice.

4. Best of all, using photographs makes children independent. Instead of relying on your verbal guidance, they come to rely on themselves. The rule is not to nag, but simply to tell your child to look at the photographs.

The evening routine

The evening routine is set up very much like the morning routine. Again you will use photographs to create a visual guide, helping your children to know what they should be doing now, and what they must do next.

Here is an example of an evening routine:

PHOTO 1: TIDY-UP TIME
By the time you set up this routine, you will already have worked on organising the bedroom. So, tidying-up time should be quite short, as it is simply a matter of putting things back into their boxes. Using the countdown to prepare your child for tidy-up time is useful here.

PHOTO 2: BATH TIME

It is often a good idea to walk with your child to the bath and make sure that they start this process. If you just shout 'Bath time!' from the kitchen while you continue to cook, you can be certain that you will find your child still glued to the TV set 20 minutes later. You are now 20 minutes behind schedule and want your child to come and eat, but they have not bathed – and so your routine does not stay consistent. At the beginning, take the child to the bathroom and actually turn on the taps. Your child will think, 'Oh well – I'm here, the water is running ... I may as well bath.'

PHOTO 3: GET READY FOR THE NEXT DAY

It is a good idea, when your children are in their bedrooms putting on their pyjamas, to get them to take out their clothes for the next day. Even if your child can reach all his or her clothes and knows where to find them, encourage them to take everything out the night before, including clean socks, underwear and jerseys. This prevents any problems in the morning when your child discovers that he or she does not have a clean white shirt or has lost his or her jersey.

During this time, homework diaries need to be checked and brought for signing, school bags need to be packed, as well as any sports kit that is needed for the next day. Have a place for these, preferably near the front door, so that your child sees them as he or she runs out of the door in the morning. This will help avoid any frantic calls from a desperate child begging you to bring his soccer boots to school, or he will be kicked off the team.

Tell your children that if they tidy up, bath and get ready for the next day quickly, then they can watch a little TV before supper. This is a carrot that you can dangle for good co-operation. However, if they take too long there won't be time for any TV, as it'll be time for supper. It is a good idea to try and have supper at the same time every day. Tidy-up time and bath time can be a bit more flexible, depending on factors such as the weather (in summer children can stay outside and play for longer, but in winter they usually come in earlier and bath to get warm, which allows for more free time before supper) or the kind of day they have had (sometimes their day has been too full, and they need to come in and have some quiet time before having supper and going to bed).

> **NOTE:**
>
> It may not be convenient for you to supervise your children getting ready for the next day during this time, as you may be too busy preparing supper. This part of the routine can be moved to after supper, or even just before your child gets into bed, if these times suit you better. Remember, everyone's routine may be different – but it is important that you establish a routine for your family and stick to it.

PHOTO 4: DINNER TIME

Dinner needs to take place at a table, not on your laps in front of the TV. Eating dinner at the table encourages discussion and allows your children more talking time in an environment where they have to learn to wait their turn and listen to others. This improves their speech and vocabulary development as well as their social skills. It also allows children to share the troubles and triumphs they've had during the day, which helps to improve their self-esteem and emotional well-being. Dinner time can be a very important bonding time for families.

PHOTO 5: ACTIVITY TIME

This slot may sound unimportant, but it can become the gem of your day. Children crave our attention, but we are often so busy running around fetching and carrying them, cooking for them and helping with homework that there is no time left for anything else. Children, unfortunately, do not see these tasks as 'quality time', and often want more from us. If we schedule this time into our day, we might just stop and make time to actually play with our children. Remember the truth of the old saying: 'A family that plays together, stays together.'

Activity time is, first and foremost, for finishing homework left over from the afternoon. This is the time when you can be available to help your child with anything he or she did not understand. However, once homework is all done, this becomes 'game time'. If you stick to this rule and actually play with your children, they will be motivated to get their homework done in the afternoon so that you do not have to battle with them to get it done in the evenings. If you promise to play games but never do, there is no motivation to do homework any earlier.

During this time we encourage you to switch off the TV and to play card games like Snap, Pick-up-Pairs, Rummy or Go Fish; board games like Snakes and Ladders, Ludo, Cluedo and Braingain, and games like Pick-up-Sticks, Backgammon, Checkers, Battleships or Bingo. If you haven't heard of some of these games or can't remember how to play them, find out – because they can be a lot of fun. These games can also become wonderful tools for enhancing your child's reading, spelling and mathematical skills (see Chapter 9 for ideas). They are also useful for developing their social skills and teaching them how to be good winners and losers. If they don't learn this at home, where will they learn it? Having a set activity time every evening also gives you a golden opportunity to spend quality time with your children.

A NOTE ON GAMES:

Many children are going into Grade 1 with poorly consolidated visual and auditory perceptual skills (the ability to make sense of what they see and hear), speech and vocabulary. They also frequently struggle to take turns and play in a co-operative way. As a result, many children now have to attend some form of therapy to make up for these deficits. One of the reasons for such difficulties is that children are losing the art of play and the perceptual and social benefits of playing games. More and more children watch too much television or spend too much time interacting with other forms of technology. Few of these activities develop any skills at all and simply turn children into couch potatoes.

The new millennium vegetable

As parents, you can make a world of difference to your child's development and social well-being by taking some time to play old-fashioned games.

PHOTO 6: BRUSH TEETH

Have you taught your child how to brush his or her teeth properly? Ask a dentist who's good with children if you are not sure how it should be done.

PHOTO 7: GO TO THE TOILET

Encourage this just before going to bed to try and prevent any accidents (yes, even older children sometimes have accidents) or having a broken night's sleep because they have to get up and go to the bathroom during the night.

PHOTO 8: INTO BED

It is really important to stick to a set bedtime. If you constantly waver and let your child go to bed at different times each evening, you will continue to have difficulty establishing a consistent bedtime. For some parents bedtime means sleep time; for others it means getting into bed, where you can listen to a story, read, or listen to some music. Whatever you agree to is OK, as long as it works for your child and does not keep them up late. Children need a good, long night's rest.

Maintaining the routines

Setting up a routine is easy. In this case it can be quite fun too, as much of it is like a photo-shoot and exhibition. Maintaining the routines over time, however, is another matter altogether.

Trouble shooting

You *will* have teething problems when setting up your routines. Your child will fight you, you will forget, you will give in, or you may need to make changes. Whatever the reason, the first three weeks of setting up a routine can be terrifying, and many parents resort to the familiar 'nag, nag, follow around and nag some more' method.

The long-term benefits of having smooth-running morning and evening routines are enormous, so hang in there. Like many things, the initial start-up is hard, but if you carry on with courage and determination the outcomes are outstanding. Instead of becoming despondent, use the first week or two to find out where your problem areas are (child dresses too slowly, for example; child doesn't like to eat breakfast; you still have to nag to get him to brush his teeth), and then target these difficulties one at a time until your routines are running smoothly. Remember that Rome wasn't built in a day, and it will take some time to establish a smooth-running routine in which your child can get ready independently (yes, without you ... except for your help in preparing breakfast and cooking supper – and they can even help with this as they get older!)

So how do we achieve a smooth-running household?

Let's look at an example:

You have taken the photos, put them up in the bedroom and kitchen, and in the correct order. Your child has posed and fawned over his own image for hours but still, after all this, he won't get dressed on time and you have to nag him to hurry, hurry, *hurry.*

What do you do?

The business of getting dressed, especially when clothes are laid out the night before, should not take any child of school-going age longer than five or six minutes; ten minutes at the most. One way to deal with children who dawdle in the morning is to use a kitchen- or an egg-timer. For getting dressed, set the timer for 10 minutes. Place it where your child can see it counting down and where she or he can hear the insistent *tick, tick, tick* ... a constant reminder that time is passing and that they need to move with a sense of urgency. This may just hurry them along. But it may not be enough, and your child may need some incentive to get dressed quickly.

Try the behaviour modification process described in Chapter 1. Remember, it takes three weeks to consolidate a habit, so it will take three weeks to teach your child how to get dressed quickly (younger children may need a bit longer).

WEEK 1: INSTANT REWARDS

For the first week tell your child that if he is dressed and ready before the timer rings, you will give him a reward. Discuss what you mean by 'getting dressed' (for example that he has to be completely dressed with socks and shoes on).

If your children still need some help, you can tell them that being dressed means having all your clothes on, but that you will then help them to do up buttons or tie shoelaces (for girls, getting dressed can even include having their hair tied up if they can manage this on their own). Also discuss 'up front' with your child what reward they will get for doing this. Some good ideas include R1 or R2 to spend at the tuck shop, or you could say to your child that if he helps you by getting dressed quickly in the mornings you will let him stay up ten minutes later tonight. (This reward costs you nothing, but can be very effective, as children love to stay up later. However, this reward can only be used if you have a strict bedtime!) Then set the timer, walk out and leave your child to get dressed. If they are dressed and ready before the timer, give them their reward. This must be done every day for at least the first week, to try and get children to make the link that it pays to get dressed quickly in this house (here you are using the principle of instant rewards). But remember that after one week your child will not have learned how to get dressed quickly. If you stop focusing on it, they will go straight back to dawdling.

WEEK 2: DELAYED REWARDS

You cannot go on rewarding children every day for getting dressed in good time, or you will soon be bankrupt. Your reward will also lose its impact. So, for the second week, tell your child that you are still going to set the timer for ten minutes, but that this week if they are dressed and ready before the bell rings you will still give them their money – or their time staying up late – but that you will save it all and give it to them on Friday. By doing this, you are teaching your child to delay gratification. This is one of the best things you can ever teach them. Many adults end up in therapy because they cannot delay gratification and end up getting themselves into all sorts of trouble.

Children need to learn that if they get an instant reward it is often small, but that if you delay gratification the rewards are often so much better. You can't buy much at the tuck shop for R2, but if you have R10 you could probably buy a hamburger and juice. You also can't do much if you stay up for ten extra minutes, but if you stay up for 50 extra minutes on Friday, that is a lot of extra playing or TV-watching time.

WEEK 3: INTERMITTENT REWARDS

This week works differently. This time you are going to give an intermittent reward. This means that you tell your child that you are still going to set the timer every morning, but that you have chosen one morning for a special surprise and you are not going to tell him which it is. If he is ready before the timer goes, then he will get the surprise. If your child cannot bear the suspense of not knowing what the surprise is, you may have to tell him – but don't say on which day he will get the reward. Then, on Monday, when your child comes running into the room to say he is ready, congratulate him but say that today is not the day of the reward. In this way your child learns another life lesson – sometimes in life we have to do things and we get nothing for it! Do the same for Tuesday and Wednesday, or until the day arrives that you have chosen for the reward (a useful tip – plan up front which day of the week suits you best). If your child is dressed before the bell on Thursday and this was the day that you had chosen for the reward, then congratulate him and tell him what his reward is – something like going for a milkshake together after school. Choose something that is a special treat and not something that you do all the time. Rewards that involve doing something together are always good.

Intermittent rewards are the best types of rewards to keep good behaviour going forever. Your child will think that it is worthwhile getting dressed quickly, just in case today is the day that there is a reward. We sometimes use intermittent rewards incorrectly by giving in to tantrums – especially in shopping centres – and this then reinforces the tantrum and maintains the unwelcome behaviour. Beware of this!

After three weeks, children should have learned that it is easy to get dressed within ten minutes in the morning, and exactly how long ten minutes is. If after three weeks, however, you never again comment on how quickly they dress or thank them for their co-operation, after a couple of weeks they will go back to their bad old ways. Continue to give intermittent rewards (not every week), and thank or compliment them on how they look, and they will continue to dress quickly from then on.

Following this method of timing children and rewarding them if they do things quickly works well for things such as dressing, bathing and even eating (but be careful, with eating, that you do not teach your children to eat too quickly. Always give them more than enough time to finish their meal, but not so long that they spend hours at the table). You can't, however, say to a child, 'If you brush your teeth within five minutes I will give you a reward.' This is not a timed task. If you are having difficulties getting your children to brush their teeth, comb their hair, tidy up or even get ready for the next day, then use a star chart to reinforce these activities. Refer to Chapter 1 if you are unsure of how to do this. Remember, when using a star chart, only to focus on one or two things at a time.

Handy hints

✍ Always link your rewards to some form of praise. For example, thank your children, hug them or tell them how smart they look when they dress quickly. In this way you are linking Level 1 and Level 2 of moral development (See Kohlberg's stages of moral development in Chapter 1), and so, when you remove the physical rewards, your children still feel good because they are getting your approval.

✍ Don't give up! Establishing a routine does not happen overnight, and it does not happen by chance. Remember that it takes three weeks to form a habit. Stick with it!

✍ Don't give up too quickly. Small children, in particular, may need longer than three weeks to consolidate good habits. They may also require additional supervision and assistance from you. If something is too difficult for children, they will stop trying even if there is a reward dangling over their heads.

✍ Remember – there is no one magical routine. Routines must be developed according to your family's needs. Creating and maintaining routines takes time and work in the beginning, but the short and long term rewards for you and your children are well worth it.

✍ You may not believe this, but children, especially boys, love rules and order. It makes them feel safe and secure in an insecure, ever-changing world. When your children challenge your rules and routines, they are not fighting the restrictions; they are testing you. If you are able to do as you say and maintain rules and routines in the face of their challenges, the message that your children will get is that Mommy or Daddy (or preferably both) are safe, and that therefore I am safe.

4 Weekly Planners

How to deal with busy afternoons

Weekly planners will help you and your child organise the time between getting home from school and the first activity in the evening routine. The main aim of these planners is to schedule specific times for homework each afternoon, and also to know where your child should be and what activities they should be doing on any given day. Planners are also useful for tracking children's activities and making sure they are not overscheduled. Overscheduled children become exhausted, grumpy, and can be defiant. It is essential for children to have 'down' time during which they can relax, play at home, and simply have some much-needed time away from rules, timers, schedules and parents.

What a weekly planner looks like

Weekly planners need to include the days of the week and be divided into half-hourly time slots. You can design them in any way you wish, but keep them:

- Big enough to write on, and,
- Easy to read.

Using a laminated or a whiteboard weekly planner is useful, since you can change them easily from one term to the next as your children's activities change.

Here is an example of a weekly planner:

WEEKLY PLANNER

Times	Monday	Tuesday	Wednesday	Thursday	Friday
School					
1:00 1:30					
1:30 2:00					
2:00 2:30					
2:30 3:00					
3:00 3:30					
3:30 4:00					
4:00 4:30					
4:30 5:00					
5:00 5:30					
5:30 6:00					
Things to remember					

Making your weekly planner

These planners are very easy to make. Either design them on a computer using tables, or simply make them on paper using a ruler and pencil. A better idea (if they are old enough or skilled enough and you have the patience) is to encourage your children to make their own weekly planners. In this way they will be invested in the process from the very beginning. It is useful to make the planners a little bigger than A4 size. A3 works really well, as the blocks are easier to write in and the chart is easy to see. You will also need a set of coloured pens with which you will fill in the planner (non-permanent pens, if you are working on laminated weekly planners or whiteboards).

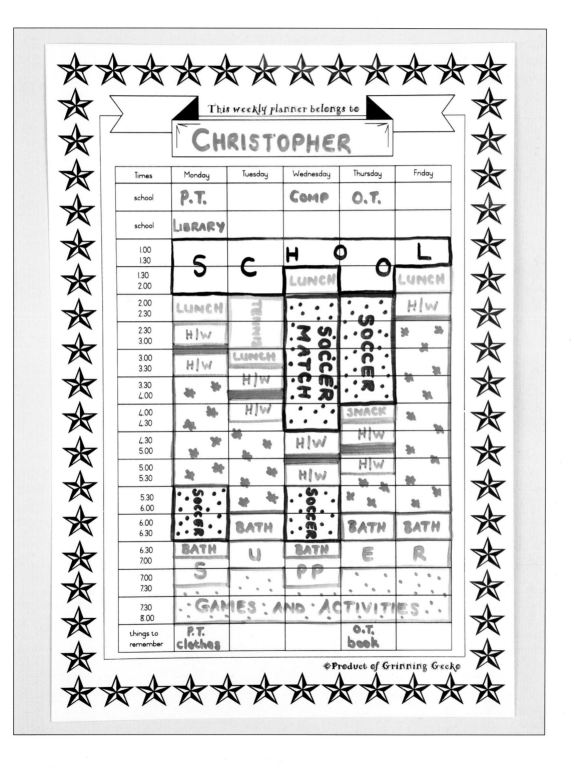

This weekly planner belongs to

CHRISTOPHER

Times	Monday	Tuesday	Wednesday	Thursday	Friday
school	P.T.		COMP	O.T.	
school	LIBRARY				
1.00 1.30	S	C	H	O	O	L
1.30 2.00			LUNCH		LUNCH
2.00 2.30	LUNCH	TENNIS	SOCCER MATCH	SOCCER	H/W
2.30 3.00	H/W				
3.00 3.30	H/W	LUNCH			
3.30 4.00		H/W			
4.00 4.30		H/W		SNACK	
4.30 5.00			H/W	H/W	
5.00 5.30			H/W	H/W	
5.30 6.00	SOCCER		SOCCER		
6.00 6.30		BATH		BATH	BATH
6.30 7.00	BATH	U	BATH	E	R
7.00 7.30	S		PP		
7.30 8.00	GAMES AND ACTIVITIES				
things to remember	P.T. clothes			O.T. book	

©Product of Grinning Gecko

Using the weekly planner

STEP 1: FILLING IN THE NON-NEGOTIABLES

These planners can only be made once the extra-mural timetable has come home from school. Allow your child to choose the extra-murals and fill these in, as well as any other fixed afternoon activities that occur at the same time every week, such as therapy sessions. Let your child choose a different colour for each of these activities.

If your child wants to do many activities, don't become hysterical.

If you immediately say 'No', your child will accuse you of being mean and horrible and you will probably end up arguing. Don't try to reason with your child. Rather say nothing and let the difficulties show themselves as you and your child fill in the planner with all the activities.

When activities start to overlap, ask your child how he or she will manage to be in two places at once. If they have two or three activities scheduled on the same day, ask them when they are going to do their homework and have free time. Children are not stupid, and will back down. A lack of homework time probably won't convince them to cut down on extra-murals, but a loss of free time will certainly get them to change their minds. In this way, you avoid fuss and drama and you create the opportunity for your child to see what the problem is. If they insist on sticking to a heavy schedule, and lose out on free time, then they have only themselves to blame.

If you have more than one child, it is important to sit and make these weekly planners together in order to establish whether it will be possible for you to get all your children to their activities at the specific times (and yes, it is important to be on time). Some compromises may be reached to suit the whole family.

STEP 2: REST, CHANGE AND EAT (LUNCH)

After filling in the non-negotiables, you then fill in the daily activities according to the time you have available. The first activity to fill in is a time to Rest, Change and Eat (RCE). Teach children that when they get home from school they are tired, and have run out of 'petrol'. Therefore they need to refuel (i.e. eat) before being able to carry on with the rest of the day. It is also really important from a physiological and cognitive point of view to give children time to 'change gear' from school to home mode and to give their bodies and brains a break before trying to cope with the demands of homework. Although there are children who prefer to start their homework immediately and get it out of the way, it is preferable if they take a break.

The amount of RCE time depends on how much time there is in the afternoon and how much homework needs to be done. If children come home straight after school, this time can be a little longer (anything from half an hour to an hour, but not longer). However, if they are getting home later after an extra-mural, their break will be much shorter. If children get home very late, for example after a swimming gala or playing a cricket match, then they have to understand that there will be no RCE time. They will have to come straight home and do their homework. Their break was the entire time that they were at their extra-mural. Weekly planners are very useful in this regard, as they allow you to see the days when your children will be home late and, therefore, to plan in advance when to send them to school with extra lunch for the day.

Fill in the RCE slots in a different colour to your non-negotiable activities.

STEP 3: HOMEWORK

Once these 'breathing spaces' have been filled in, you fill in homework time, once again in another colour. (Many children choose black – the colour of doom and gloom!) Getting homework done is a huge battlefield in many families, and can be the cause of serious relationship problems between parents and children.

Getting homework done is discussed in detail in Chapter 7, but in the meantime, homework time needs to be scheduled onto the weekly planner. Homework must always follow RCE time. Teach your children that *work before play* makes for a happy day. If they play first, they spend the whole afternoon with their homework hanging over their heads and actually spoiling their fun. The quicker the homework is over and done with, the better.

Sit there, and DON'T MOVE until you have finished!

The weekly planner can also be used to teach children to work 'smarter', not necessarily longer. We usually tell our children that they must go and sit at their desks and not get up until all their homework is done.

This is often because it can be so difficult to get children to their desks in the first place; we are desperate to get them to stay. What is ironic in these situations, however, is that the longer children stay at their desks without a break, the longer it takes them to complete even a small amount of homework.

If children are not allowed to take a physical break from their desks, their brains are forced to take some 'concentration downtime'. This can be in the form of daydreaming, doodling or staring blankly out of the window. Another type of break involves becoming distracted by stationery or any toys that are lying around. A third form of break includes going to the toilet (even when unnecessary), or insisting on needing a calculator (or dictionary, or whatever else) which is in another room. These 'breaks' don't happen because your child is naughty and lazy; they happen in direct response to the demands of the brain and are largely uncontrollable.

To avoid these time-wasting breaks, rather schedule in some *real* breaks during homework time. The best is to encourage children to work for about 25 minutes and then to take a 10-minute break ('steal' five minutes from the end one half-hour slot and five minutes from the beginning of the next slot). After the break they must work for another 25 minutes. In this way children work a '50-minute-hour' and, although they spend less time working because of the break, they use the time efficiently and get more work done.

Some children may need another 25-minute slot to complete their homework, especially in their later primary school years and once they reach high school. It is, however, not wise for children to work for more than four 25-minute slots without having a long break. Remember children need 'down' time, even when they are older. By now you should also have set up your evening routine, which includes an 'activity' time which can be used to finish homework.

STEP 4: FREE TIME
Colour all the remaining slots in your child's favourite colour. This is free time. During this time they can choose what they would like to do (within reason, of course).

You can still have some say in what they are allowed to do, but be careful of being too prescriptive. It is *not* all right for children to sit in front of the television for three hours or to play TV games all afternoon (after reading Chapter 9, you may actually choose to sell your television); but at the same time don't force them to play educational games all afternoon. These can be played during the activity time in your evening routine, when the whole family can get involved.

But we only get home at five o'clock!

If you are at work until 5pm and your children are at aftercare, homework should be completed before you collect them. If it is not being done, you will need to discuss this with your child's aftercare teacher, as the children cannot get home late and then have to sit down to do homework. When you get home you should kick straight into your evening routine.

If your child is at home in the afternoon with a caregiver while you are at work, it is imperative to set up a weekly planner and insist that your child follows the plan. Your caregiver will have to assist you in this regard. Don't allow your children to tell you that they need your help to do homework.

There will always be work that they can do on their own. Any work that really needs your assistance can be kept aside until you get home, and will have to be done during the activity time in your evening routine. Remind your children that they don't get to play games or watch television in the evenings until all their homework is done. This is often a good motivating factor for them to get their work done on their own.

If you get home late because your children have been busy with extra-murals all afternoon, then this becomes a problem. You need to check that you are not trying to cram too much into their day. If you can't change anything, then encourage your children to try and do some homework during any spare time that they have during the school morning (i.e. if they finish some of their work early in class and have a few minutes to spare before the bell rings). Another useful tip is to keep a spare pencil case and a clipboard (a bigger board is even more useful) in your car and to encourage your children to start some of their homework in the car while you are waiting for siblings to finish their activities.

Handy hints

✍ Try to schedule homework time as early in the afternoon as possible, especially if you have a young child.

✍ Do not schedule homework time during a child's favourite television programme or when the rest of the family is relaxing. This will guarantee that homework will be a battle you will not win.

✍ Try not to keep too much homework for after supper, as your child will have a full tummy and will often feel sleepy. If your child does have to do some homework after supper, sit with him or her and help in whichever way you can without actually doing the work for them. In this way you will be able to get the work done faster and get your child off to bed at the correct time.

✍ The weekly planner is more flexible in terms of time than the evening and morning routines because of the variety of activities and appointments that have to be done in the afternoon, like extra-murals, haircuts, visits to the dentist and so on. Even if the times change from day to day, try and get the sequence of activities the same, these being Rest, Change and Eat time (RCE), homework time and play time.

✍ The ability to plan and organise a day is a time-management life skill that will benefit your children enormously as they get older and their lives become more and more busy.

5 Monthly Planners

> Why have you left this project until the last minute?

> What do you mean you have a meeting? It's the school play tonight!

> I can't take you to a party **and** your sister to swimming!

> I can't believe I forgot my anniversary!

> I'm so sorry I missed the meeting – I was at my child's gala, and it completely slipped my mind!

Getting the BIG PICTURE

Monthly planners are simply monthly calendars on which you write down all the events and activities that involve the members of your family over a three-month period.

Monthly planners give you the 'big picture' or overview of upcoming activities and events. By writing down all your future events and activities, you will avoid last-minute panics, such as forgetting that there is a project to hand in or that you still have to buy your mother-in-law's birthday present. Monthly planners can be the saving grace of a big, busy family.

> Isn't it Parents' Meeting tonight?

Why use monthly planners?

Writing down all the activities and events your family members have to remember helps to streamline family life and ensures that you don't miss important functions.

Monthly planners also help you avoid the dreaded and embarrassing double-booking drama.

Hi, I'm so sorry, but we can't make Ginny's party this afternoon. I feel like such an idiot, but I've just remembered we have another party. Yes ... yes, I know you catered and made party packs for everyone, it's just that ... Hello ... hello?

Moreover, monthly planners are great for minimising the paper clutter that has been known to completely overwhelm fridges before moving on to colonise other kitchen surface areas, if not the whole house.

Too much disorganised paper clutter wastes huge amounts of time and creates frustration.

Where did I put that invitation? Who took the invitation? I don't know how to get there and now we are going to be late. For goodness sake help me, don't just stand there!

By the time the offending invitation has been tracked down under an old newsletter on the fridge, your children are quivering nervous wrecks, you have become a potential murderer, and the very idea of having fun at a party is making you all feel ill.

Using monthly planners will help you avoid all these embarrassing and stressful situations and help you lead a calmer, more organised life.

Preparing your monthly planners

a. Monthly planners must always have enough space for at least four activities each day – A3 is a good size.

b. Monthly planners will eventually be thrown away, so don't invest too heavily in what they look like or the material from which they are made. They need to be practical, not decorative.
c. Avoid laminated or whiteboard monthly planners, because it is too easy to smudge or erase upcoming activities, either accidentally or on purpose.

What information goes onto monthly planners?

The types of activities and events that are recorded on monthly planners are school holidays, public holidays, anniversaries, birthdays, birthday parties, play dates, sports matches, deadlines for projects, tests and exams, school outings, school plays, special days at school, tuck days, appointments for haircuts, dentists, orthodontists, parents' evening and civvies days. (How many times has your tearful and hugely embarrassed child arrived at school in uniform on a civvies day?)

You can also include your own work events such as presentations, after-hours meetings, cocktail parties and dinner or movie dates. Fun activities like TV shows you don't want to miss can also be included. By now you'll be getting the picture that your very lives can be written down on these planners.

Certain activities need a bit more detail. For example, as soon as a party invitation comes home, fill in the date, address and contact number on the monthly planner and throw the invitation away. In this way, all important dates and back-up information such as addresses and contact numbers are centralised, and you can start getting rid of the colonies of paper that clutter up your house, confuse your mind and confound your life.

Monthly planners are for reminding you about one-off events, so there is no need to include information like regular soccer practice. This type of routine activity will go onto the weekly planner.

Three months at a glance

Three-monthly planners (for example March, April and May) need to be on view at a time, which will give you an overview of what's coming up over the next three months. These planners should be placed either top-to-bottom (works well for the fridge) or side-by-side. The reason for this is to improve forward planning.

If you show only one calendar month at a time you can't see the following months, and run the risk of forgetting – and therefore not planning for – important dates. Also, it is surprisingly easy to forget to flip a calendar from one month to the next.

THREE MONTHS AT A GLANCE

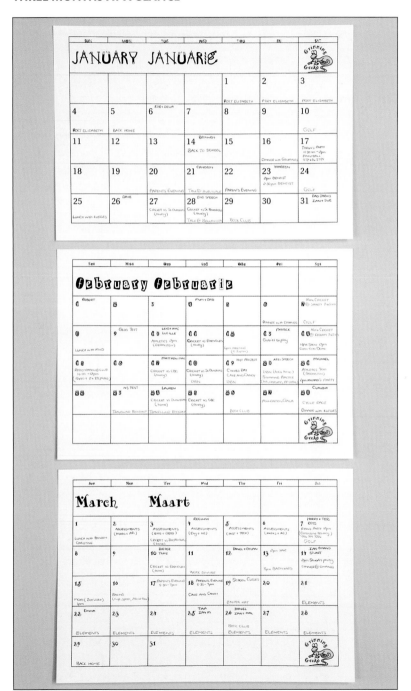

A typical three-monthly plannner layout

So often we remember a few days late to change the month, and – lo and behold – we have missed another dentist's appointment!

While showing one calendar month is too limited, don't try to become an organisational superhero and show all 12 months at once. This will probably completely overwhelm you.

Keeping the monthly planners up to date

It is also important that as soon as one month finishes, you should remove it and move the next two months up or along, and add the new month. Don't just keep adding new months while leaving the old ones up. You will miss the point of using these monthly planners, and your friends will think that you have wallpapered your kitchen with calendars – not a good décor move! File the finished months for a year before you throw them out, just in case you need to refer back to something.

Using colour to organise

MONTHLY PLANNER

SUN	MON	TUE	WED	THU	FRI	SAT
JANUARY JANUARIE						Grinning Gecko
				1 PORT ELIZABETH	2 PORT ELIZABETH	3 PORT ELIZABETH
4 PORT ELIZABETH	5 BACK HOME	6 ROB + DELIA	7	8	9	10 GOLF
11	12	13	14 BRONWEN BACK TO SCHOOL	15	16 DINNER WITH GRUPPINGS	17 TYRON'S PARTY 11:30am – 2pm PAINTBALL
18	19	20 PARENTS EVENING	21 CAMERON TALK @ HURLYVALE	22 PARENTS EVENING	23 WARREN 2pm DENTIST 2:30 DENTIST	24 GOLF
25 LUNCH WITH KLESSES	26 DAVE	27 CRICKET VS ST DUNSTANS (a)	28 ENG SPEECH CRICKET VS ST BENEDICTS (a)	29 BOOK CLUB	30	31 DAD JARVIS IAN + SUE

As all members of the family should be filling in their own important dates, the planners tend to get quite full. If they are not used according to a plan, complete chaos can result.

Your best bet is to allocate a different-coloured pen to each member of the family. Make sure these pens live close to, or are even tied to, the monthly planners, and that they are never moved.

Who fills in monthly planners?

Monthly planners are an ongoing process, and fill up as and when new dates and appointments enter your lives. The older family members should take responsibility for filling in their own dates. For the younger members of the family, an adult will have to do the writing, but make sure you involve the child and explain what you are doing. Young children learn a lot from monthly planners; not only planning and organisation, but the idea of days, weeks and months. Concepts such as 'in two days' time', 'last week' or even 'three more sleeps' which can be very confusing for some children, can also be easily explained and understood with the aid of the planners.

Handy hints

✍ Build five minutes into your evening routine for monthly planner updates when the whole family is around. Just after supper is a good time.

✍ You must consult your weekly planner when making once-off appointments e.g. dentist appointments or haircuts, so that there are no clashes with fixed appointments such as sports practices or therapy sessions.

✍ As with all new routines and structures, the first few weeks can be trying, and there will be teething problems. This is normal, and doesn't mean you are a failure. Persevere until filling in the planners becomes a habit, because once they work you will never know how you managed without them.

6 The Ultimate Homework Diary

> The homework diary never comes home. I never know what we are supposed to be doing.

> Where's the newsletter?

> You haven't written down any homework at all!

> What have you done with your homework diary – all these pages are stuck together with some disgusting sticky ... is this jam?

> What do you mean you need another diary? Have you lost yours?

> You've just written 'maths' here. What maths?

Getting homework home, done and back to school

As you are probably aware, the homework diary, that little book that holds so much promise for order and organisation, can frequently be the flint that sparks off the most unforgettable and regrettable fights between you and your child. Often, homework is either:

a. Not written down at all.

> There's nothing written down here. Don't you have any homework?

> Um, no ...

b.   Written down too briefly.

c.   Written down under the wrong day or month.

d.   Or indecipherable.

'Take out your diaries and write down your homework.' So easy to say – but have you ever stopped to consider the dangers lurking in this simple instruction that are waiting to trip up your child?

For starters, 'Take out your diary' is actually a bit more complicated than it sounds.

Your child has to:

- Open his or her school case, which is often a great big lug of a bag which has to be hauled onto the desk, or one of those wheelie-bags which is probably parked out of the way, and which your child has to go and fetch.

- Rifle through the flotsam and jetsam in the bag to locate the dreaded diary which, often being small, filters to the bottom along with the mouldy sweet papers and a two-month supply of newsletters.

- Open the diary to the right month, date and day – the triple whammy!

'Write down your homework' is even more complicated. Your child has to:

- Find something with which to write.

- Copy the homework off the board (What if your child writes slowly? What if he or she can't see the board clearly?)

- Often teachers give homework instructions verbally, which means your child has to listen to, understand, summarise and write down the relevant information. (What if the class is noisy? What if the bell rings as the teacher is speaking?)

- The relevant books or worksheets must then be packed into the school bag and the homework diary returned to the bag.

- To top it all, these steps have to be done accurately, speedily and neatly in the final frantic five minutes of a lesson when all your child can think about is packing up and moving on to the next lesson, where the process will probably begin all over again.

Considering the complexities inherent in the seemingly simple statement, 'Take out your diaries and write down your homework,' the next time your little one brings home instructions that resemble broken telephone conversations – garbled, muddled and incoherent – stop and think about why this has happened before you start bellowing like an enraged bull!

Traditional homework diaries

Although schoolchildren all have homework diaries, these are often too small to be effective, or do not have enough structure to help children learn planning and organisational skills.

To add to the burden of homework, frequently children also have to deal with 'administrative' information such as newsletters, notices and invitations – where do these go? Homework diaries are often too small to hold these pieces of paper, which is why they end up mauled, scrunched and covered in jam and crumbs at the bottom of the school bag ready for you to discover a month later.

As you can see, the co-ordination of homework is complicated, detailed and fraught with obstacles over which your child will inevitably stumble and fall. But don't worry, there is hope. Hope on its own, however, is not good enough. You need a plan – and that is where the Ultimate Homework Diary comes in!

The Ultimate Homework Diary
(Adapted from the work of John F. Taylor)

The Ultimate Homework Diary is a system that helps children (and parents) cope with the many details that have to be co-ordinated between home and school. This diary is like an 'IN tray, OUT tray' and FILING system, and will encourage your child to centralise information into one well-organised file.

To make the diary you will need:

- A large preferably three- or four-ring binder file.
- Four A4 file dividers in different colours.
- Coloured plastic A4 envelopes in three different shades. These colours need to be the same as three of the above file dividers (you will need between one and three of each colour, depending on how much homework your child brings home).
- Plastic filing pockets.
- A zip-fastened pencil bag (fabric or thin plastic).
- A bulldog clip.

1. THE FILE

The file must be sturdy, because it will be in constant use. A hard-covered file is recommended, but as children get older they sometimes complain that the file is too heavy, so you may want to buy a good quality plastic-covered file. Let your child choose a file with a 'cool' picture, or decorate their file with their favourite photos, pictures or stickers. This file belongs to your child, so don't prescribe what the cover should look like.

Three- or four-ring binder files are also preferable, as there is less chance of all the clips opening if the file is dropped. A two-ring binder opens easily if dropped, and then everything spills all over the floor.

This file does not always have to be put in your child's school bag. It can simply be carried around from class to class. It may even be a good idea to have a separate bag (just a bit bigger than the file) to slip the file into, in order to protect it and to prevent anything from falling out. The file then becomes your child's 'life'. They have to make sure that they take it to school in the morning and that they bring it home in the afternoon. If they have their file, they should always have everything with them that they need to do their work.

2. THE CONTENTS

a.   The 'week-at-a-glance' homework sheet (example on facing page)

This homework sheet is more detailed than a traditional homework diary. It encourages weekly planning and scheduling, and is also a constant reminder of long-term assignments and tests. The homework sheets must be replaced weekly. Sometime over the weekend (it is recommended that you make this a set time, in order not to forget), sit with your child and go through the sheet. Check that whatever had to be done is done, and don't forget to carry over long-term tests and assignments. (The long-term tests and assignments also need to be recorded on the monthly planners – see Chapter 5.) By replacing the sheet each week, your child will not be

HOMEWORK SHEET

Name: _____   Week of: _____   to _____

Subject	Monday	Tuesday	Wednesday	Thursday

Parent's Signature	
Mon	
Tues	
Wed	
Thurs	

TAKE TO SCHOOL:

Mon _____
Tues _____
Wed _____
Thurs _____
Fri _____

BRING HOME:

Mon _____
Tues _____
Wed _____
Thurs _____
Fri _____

Tests

Date	Subject

Assignments

Due Date	Subject

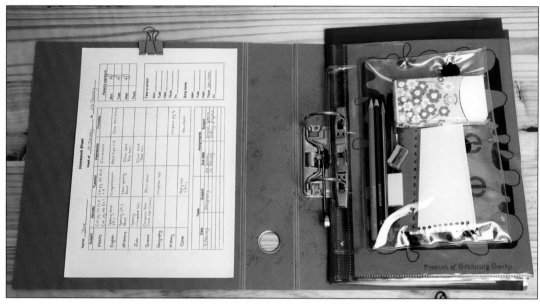

The Ultimate Homework Diary

overwhelmed with and confused by old information. The colour is important, as colour draws attention. Use a different colour each week. If it makes you feel better, you can store the old homework sheets in a separate file, rather than throwing them away. In this way they will be available to refer back to if necessary. Don't store them for too long, though, as this just creates clutter. They can probably be thrown away at the end of each term.

b.   The pencil case
Pencil cases can cause more trouble than you would ever believe possible.

In Chapter 7 there is detailed information on managing stationery for homework. But pencil cases and stationery also manage to go walkabout at school.

This is easily solved by actually punching and filing the pencil case into the Ultimate Homework Diary. In this way your child does not take out a pencil case, but only takes out the stationery that he or she needs for the lesson. Most importantly, far less can go wrong.

By attaching the pencil case to the diary, you lessen the chance of it being left lying around the school somewhere or being lost or stolen.

This pencil case is a working pencil case. Only the absolute basics are kept in it. Although your son may tell you that he needs a metre-long, luminous pencil case filled with enough equipment to make a jet engine, or your daughter demands pink feathered pencils with matching eraser and sharpener, they really do not need these fat pencil bags filled with distractions. All that children need to accomplish most of their schoolwork are:

- Two blue pens (or whatever colour the school insists that they write in).
- Two HB lead pencils.
- A plain sharpener.
- A plain eraser.

- A ruler.
- Two coloured pencils/pens (for underlining or filling in answers, and if allowed to use colour).
- A highlighter (for older children, and only if they are allowed to use these in class).
- Tissues.
- A small spiral-bound notebook.

The tissues are essential, because children often have sweaty or grubby hands after break, which need a wipe. Also, having a runny nose and having to sniff constantly has a massive impact on concentration, so tissues must be readily at hand, especially when your children are not feeling well.

The little notebook is encouraged as a way of teaching children how to make reminder lists. So, if they hear a notice over the intercom or suddenly remember that they want to tell their friend something important, instead of trying to remember it and not focusing on the lesson, teach them to write it down in the notebook. It is a fact that if we think about something and then write it down, we have a much better chance of remembering it; sometimes without even having to refer back to the note. But the note is always available in case you do forget. It is useful to keep the notebook in the working pencil case so that it is always readily available to jot down reminders.

In addition to the working pencil case, you will need two additional pencil cases for the extra stationery. One is used for scissors and glue. As your child gets older and begins to use calculators and maths sets, these are also included in this case. This is the equipment bag. The third pencil case is used to keep the rest of the coloured pencils in. As children get older they do less and less colouring in, but still need coloured pencils for some lessons. These other two bags, which contain the 'fun' things, are only to be brought out when needed, because they have a tendency to distract children. It is, after all, a lot more fun to see if you can write words on your calculator or to see how far you can stretch your nostrils with your scissors than to do long division.

c.   The three main sections
After the pencil case has been put in, the file is divided into three main sections – each containing a labelled file divider and an accompanying punched plastic envelope, preferably in the same colour as the divider.

SECTION 1: THE 'IN' TRAY
This section is the 'in' tray, but can be labelled either 'Work to be Done' or 'To Do', depending on what makes the most sense to your child.

This is the school-to-home section. Whatever needs to come home from school is placed in this section. As soon as homework is written onto the homework sheet in the front of the file, so the accompanying exercise books, textbook and/or worksheets are packed into the plastic envelope. Newsletters, notices and invitations also go into this section.

In this way, all home-bound information is put into one envelope and can't go wandering off. If your child gets lots of homework or has lots of books that need to come home to do homework, you may need one or two more of these envelopes; but remember to keep them all the same colour.

The Ultimate Homework Diary has 3 sections: Work to be done, Completed Work and Papers to Save

SECTION 2: THE 'OUT' TRAY

This section can also be called the 'Completed Work' section. This is the home-to-school section. As soon as each homework task is finished, the exercise book, textbooks and/or worksheets are packed straight back into this section so that they do not get left behind by mistake. Any money, notices and letters for the teacher also go in here so that your child sees them at school the next day and remembers to hand them in.

SECTION 3: PAPERS TO SAVE (A.K.A. 'FILE 13')

This is the section in which indefinable things are stored, such as old tests, project instructions and, in general, anything that doesn't appear to have a specific place. This envelope should be cleared out once a week. If neither you nor your child is sure what to do with the papers that are in this envelope, put them in the 'out' tray, with a note asking for help from the teacher.

d. Study guides and summaries

Study guides, summaries and anything else that can help your child with homework are filed in plastic sleeves at the back of the Ultimate Homework Diary. The reason for this is so that children do not get stuck trying to find out how to spell a word, work out a times-table sum, search for the definition of a noun or hunt down the formula for Area in their maths book. Section 4 is, in fact, an 'easy reference' section.

Examples of things that can be included in this section are:

- A summary page of the four main maths calculations (i.e. addition, subtraction, multiplication and division).
- A multiplication tables grid for quick reference.
- A summary page of shapes and their definitions.
- A summary page of mathematical formulas or conversions.
- Afrikaans language lists such as *meervoude* (plurals), *verkleinwoorde* (diminutives) or *trappe van vergelyking* (degrees of comparison).
- Other language word lists for translations.
- Definitions and examples of parts of speech.
- Study summaries (See Chapter 8).

As you can see, the Ultimate Homework Diary is structured, but simple. It centralises and organises the bits and pieces of information that continually bombard your child, instead of fragmenting them even further. In short, they are exceptional, and no child should be without one.

Handy hints

✐ Discuss the use of an Ultimate Homework Diary with your child's teacher first. Don't make one and send your child along to explain this new-fangled device to the teacher without forewarning.

✐ The diaries can be adapted to suit your child's specific needs and to fit the requirements of the school (i.e. if the school insists that your child uses their homework diary, this can then be clipped into the front of the file instead of using a homework sheet. A smaller version of the homework sheet can be photocopied and glued into the diary).

✐ In the beginning, help your child understand how to use the diary, but gradually give the responsibility over to your child, because the ultimate goal of the Ultimate Homework Diary (hence its name) is to develop your child's planning and organisational skills and to teach them to become more independent with regard to their work.

7 Making homework a habit

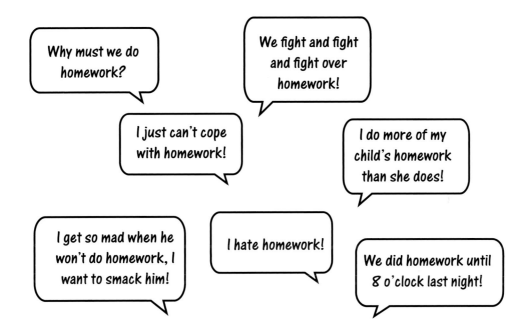

Teaching your child to 'just do it'!

Getting homework done is perhaps one of the biggest causes of strife in a family, and can cause serious rifts in relationships between parents and their children. Except for the few children who enjoy homework and finish it effortlessly, homework for most children is a painful, boring chore. Many children (and their parents) wonder continually about the benefits of homework. Despite it often being an irritation, it does have one overriding benefit – that of developing the self-discipline and integrity to do what you don't want to do, an invaluable life skill. Homework therefore becomes a vehicle for long-term learning, and if it is tackled in an organised and well-planned way, it can be done efficiently and with little fuss. The trick is to make doing homework a habit.

Preparing for homework: Laying the foundations of success

WHEN: SCHEDULING A DAILY HOMEWORK TIME
By now your child's daily homework times should already be filled in on the Weekly Planner (see Chapter 4).

Scheduling regular homework slots is important in order to establish the homework habit, so that your child knows what time homework starts and finishes each day. Having a set amount of time for homework is useful because children can see a beginning and, more importantly, an end to homework. Do not let your child start homework when she/he feels like it, because it will never get done. Homework also does not necesssarily have to be done at the same time every day. This is because children often take part in extra-mural activities that finish at different times each day. It is, however, important that homework is done at the *same* time every Monday, every Tuesday and so on.

LATER THAT EVENING ...

WHERE: THE HOMEWORK SETTING

Remember that most children consider homework boring and, as such, they are very, very susceptible to distractions during this time. You may have noticed that as homework time approaches anything and everything – except homework, that is – takes on the most fascinating flavour.

It is, therefore, really important to find a place where your child will do homework that is away from the constant distractions of the hustle and bustle of home life. Ideally, homework should be done in your child's bedroom or in a quiet part of the house which is as distraction-free as possible; a study, for example. Your child must do his or her homework in that same place every day as a way of strengthening the homework habit. It is also important to have only one child per room during homework, otherwise they tend to distract each other.

HOMEWORK SHOULD NOT BE DONE:

- On the lounge floor in front of the TV. There is no way that homework can compete with a fun TV programme. This will waste time.

- At the kitchen table when you are preparing supper.

- At the dining-room table where there may be other people, as well as many other far more entertaining distractions.

- On the bed. This leads to dozing off, rather than getting the job done.

- Don't let your child's pets into the homework room – because playing with the cat, chatting to your rat or scratching your dog's tummy are activities infinitely preferable to long division.

The working space

Once you have found a place to do homework, you need to make sure that it is properly equipped, as the right 'tools of the trade' always make work easier.

The desk and chair

Your child must sit upright at a desk. The desk and chair must be at the correct height for the child. Desks and chairs that are too small or too big affect concentration, as your child will soon become uncomfortable and start to move around restlessly. Don't buy desks and chairs that your child will 'grow into', as you will cause more harm than good. Rather invest in bigger and bigger desks and chairs as your child grows, or see if you can buy adjustable furniture. This is not always possible, as it can become an expensive exercise. If you can only buy one desk, buy it a little bigger but make sure that the chair is the correct height for the desk (i.e. that your child is not having to stretch up to reach the desk). You can always put a box under your child's feet to prevent them from dangling in the air.

This set-up is too big. A problem that will probably arise is that your child will not have a core centre of balance, and will have to spend effort and energy on balancing and stabilising the body rather than on homework. This position is also stressful on the neck and shoulders, which will quickly tire. Another point is that your child will probably prop him or herself up by placing the non-dominant hand on the chair next to the body. This means your child will not be able to use both hands to write and stabilise the page, which slows writing down and makes work messy

This desk is too small. It will result in a sore back and poor stability, as the feet cannot be used for balance. A child will be very uncomfortable working hunched over like this and will quickly lose concentration

The desk on the left is the right size. Knees are bent at right angles and feet can be placed flat on the floor. Arms are bent at right angles at the elbows and hands rest squarely on the desk. This is the ideal position in which to work

MORE HANDY ADVICE

Chairs need to have a high back to support an upright sitting position. Stools are not a good idea for comfort while doing homework.

In addition, desks must not be too narrow or too wide.

A narrow desk means you can't place a workbook, stationery and a homework book or reference book in an organised way, and books will tend to overlap each other

A too-wide desk means that stationery or books tend to move out of reach, and children have to stand up, lean or really stretch to reach what they need

Avoid, at all costs, desks with lids that lift up. These create unbelievable chaos and disorder.

IT IS A GOOD IDEA TO HAVE A DESK WITH TWO OR THREE DRAWERS

In the top drawer you can keep a spare set of the stationery that is essential for homework.

In the second drawer you can keep spare paper for doing rough work and writing study notes, etc.

If there is a third drawer, you can put reference books such as a dictionary or atlas in it.

Lighting

The desk must be well lit, so that children can see their homework books with no distracting glare or shadows.

WHAT TO AVOID

Fluorescent lighting

This is very harsh on the eyes, and tends to make a buzzing noise which can be extremely distracting to children who are sensitive to noise.

Direct sunlight

This causes a blinding glare on the page, and can make eyes water. It also becomes very hot, even in winter.

Lights from behind

Backlighting causes the hands and body to cast shadows. Your child may distract him or herself by moving around to avoid shadows falling on his or her work. This is particularly irritating when trying to write.

Dim lighting, for example from a bedside lamp

This causes sore, red eyes and possibly headaches as your child strains to see the page.

A low lamp that throws a small puddle of light

In this case only the page is illuminated and the other tools like pens, pencils and other books become lost in the dark. This also causes eye strain, as the eyes are constantly adjusting between the contrasting light and dark areas on the desk.

Lights with ceiling fans

These cause constantly moving shadows or flickering on the page.

IDEAL LIGHTING

As we have already mentioned, it is best for children to do their homework early in the afternoon. In this way they will also be able to work in natural light. If they are working at night and need additional lighting, then the best option is light that comes from above their work, so that no shadows are cast. The light can be fixed on the wall above their desk and angled to shine down on the desk. If this is not possible, then it is recommended that you buy two desk lights – but get the type with clips for attaching to a table. Two lamps may sound a bit extravagant, but consider this an investment for the rest of your child's educational career – because, as they get older, they will have to start working later into the night. These lamps are then clipped on either side of the desk and angled across the table to provide lovely bright lighting with no shadows (the two lamps cancel out each other's shadows).

Ideal lighting

Other useful homework tools

A DUSTBIN UNDER THE DESK

This may seem ridiculous, but imagine that your son needs to sharpen a pencil and that there is no dustbin under the desk or in the room. He will have to leave the work area and move to a dustbin. If the only available dustbin is in the kitchen, he will move there, sharpen the pencil and, on the way, check the fridge for juice, raid the biscuit tin, or decide to go to the toilet. By this stage the homework 'flow' has been diverted, your son has wasted time, and he has been completely distracted by other things.

Stationery

There is little point in your child sitting down on the perfect chair, at a perfect desk, and switching on the ideal lighting if the tools for the job are lacking. The tools in this case are the books and stationery necessary to do homework. One of the most common complaints heard from parents is that books and pencil bags are left at school, and this creates problems when trying to do homework. The issue of leaving books and stationery at school was dealt with in Chapter 6 and, if your child is using the Ultimate Homework Diary, books and stationery should be travelling between home and school quite smoothly.

To be on the safe side though, it is always useful to have a back-up set of stationery so that when the pencil bag is accidentally forgotten at school (and this *will* happen), it does not become an issue to fight over or an obstacle to homework. The back-up stationery must be stored in the top drawer of the desk and only used for homework. (You may not go digging in your child's stationery drawer when you urgently need a pair of scissors and you can't find your own. Your stationery must be organised in your own drawer.)

ORGANISING THE STATIONERY

Stationery can be a major distraction. Fiddling with pens and pencils, choosing colours with which to underline headings, making glue spider webs over the glue lid, tapping on the calculator, sticking bits of sticky tape over one's mouth and colouring in one's fingernails with red Koki pen are all preferable to settling down to homework. In an effort to remove these distractions, try to limit the amount of stationery available for homework to the absolute essentials, and don't keep any of it on the desk. It must be in a drawer.

THE ESSENTIAL HOMEWORK STATIONERY KIT

- **Two plain blue pens (or whatever colour the school insists that they work in):** two pens, in case one stops working. This prevents your child from scribbling on surfaces to get the ink running, which is a wonderful time-waster.

- **A few plain HB pencils that must be long enough to hold easily:** No tiny pencil stubs, no fancy, feathery, glittery pencils – because your child will spend time admiring the finery of the pencil instead of using it for its intended purpose – work. Also no huge, gimmicky pencils, tiny pencils, or anything that is not absolutely practical.

- **30cm ruler:** Again, as plain as possible, with the correct measurement units (millimetres and centimetres), which must be clearly visible.

- **Plain sharpener that works:** Barrel-type sharpeners with casings to catch the shavings are great.

- **Plain eraser that actually erases:** Fancy erasers or ones that are fragranced not only cause distraction, but often don't work efficiently. The last thing you want is your child wailing because she has rubbed a hole through a page in her maths book or made a dirty mark on the page.

- **Two coloured pens:** These are used to underline headings. Have just two, to limit choice and save time. If your child's school does not allow coloured ink for anything, leave them out.

- **A set of 12 coloured pencils:** Avoid the huge pencil-crayon sets, as they provide too much choice and can be difficult to store. Homework does not need an artist's palette; just the basics.

- **Additional stationery:** You also need a glue stick and a pair of scissors. As your child gets older and starts to use a calculator and a maths set, you may include these if you can afford an extra one of each. (Children seldom need sticky tape, staplers or a punch for school, so rather leave these out.)

Put these essentials in a cutlery organiser in the top drawer of the desk. This way your child can open the drawer and everything they need will be easily available and, very importantly, easy and quick to pack away.

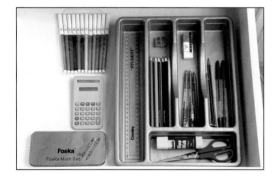 

Stationery such as wax crayons, Koki pens, paints, pastels and novelty pens and pencils must be stored away from the homework desk (see Chapter 2 – Keeping the Room Tidy). These items are rarely used for homework, and having them on or around the desk will cause clutter and distraction.

On your marks, get set – GO!

How to get homework done

By now you are organised – you have the place, the desk, the chair, the lighting and the tools. Finally it is time to actually begin doing the homework.

STEP 1

- Take out your child's homework diary and, together, check what there is for homework. Do this every day with your child, even once they have mastered the homework process and no longer need you to help them. In this way there will never be any nasty surprises – like an oral that is left for the night before it is due, or a test for which no study has been done.
- Get your child to categorise their homework into work that is 'fun' or 'boring'; 'easy' or 'difficult'; 'nice' or 'horrible' – and then decide in which order the work will be done.
- People often recommend that you start with something 'horrible' or 'difficult', and get it over with first. However, if you get bogged down with something that you do not enjoy or find difficult, you will not be motivated to do any further work. It is better for children to start their homework with something 'fun' or 'easy', and to complete this quickly. In this way they may be more inclined to attempt the next task.
- Number the homework in the order in which your child wants it to be done. This can be done on the actual homework sheet or on a separate piece of paper (Post-it notes are very useful), which is then kept on one side of the homework desk.
- When deciding the order of tasks, remember to rotate them (i.e. something 'fun' first, then something 'horrible'; then something fun again or something easy; something difficult and then something easy).
- Tasks can also be broken down into smaller, more manageable bits. For example, if a child has ten sums for maths or two different exercises, he or she can do five sums or one exercise first, move on to something else, and later in the session come back and finish the other five sums or the other exercise. This is particularly useful for children who have attention difficulties.

- It is also useful to write down the approximate time it should take to complete each task. This is a time management skill and makes homework time precise and contained. Having no time limits makes homework seem like an open-ended nightmare.
- Remember to schedule a break into the homework time as well.

STEP 2
- Get your child to take out all the books that are needed to do the homework. These can be piled on the floor or even laid out on the bed, if it is within easy reach. Don't let your child pile their books up on the desk. This just clutters the desk, and adds an element of distraction.
- Get your child to consult their homework list and check what has to be done first, then take out the books and stationery needed to complete the first task, and place them on the desk.

STEP 3
- Once your child has placed all they need to complete the first task on their desk, they may begin.
- Some children find it useful to have a timer to help them stick to the allotted time for the task. But some children become distracted by the ticking of a timer and others anxious in case they do not finish on time. In such cases, timers are clearly not useful.
- If your child likes to use a timer but does not always finish their work within the allotted time, encourage them to finish the sentence or sum they are busy with and then to note at the end of their homework list what is still outstanding. They can complete this at the end of the homework session.

STEP 4
- Once your child finishes the first task on the list, they tick it off. This gives a sense of satisfaction, and is a visual reminder that progress is being made and that the end is getting closer.

STEP 5
- Your child then puts the completed work into the 'completed work' section of the Ultimate Homework Diary, or on a new pile to be packed into their school bag later.
- They then consult their homework list and take out the books needed for the next task. Before starting this task, remember to take out any additional stationery that may be required or to pack away stationery that won't be needed for that specific task. In this way you teach children to always limit their distractions. Stationery items make wonderful toys!

STEP 6
- Your child continues ticking off work done and consulting the homework list until all the work is done.
- The final step is to bring their homework diary for signing (or to put it in a specific place that has been agreed by both of you for you to sign when you get home from work). Anything that they may require help with can be put in the same place as the homework diary, so that it is all easily accessible once you are available to help them.
- Your child must then re-pack their schoolbag and put all the stationery back into the top drawer to be used again tomorrow.

Trouble-shooting

Because many homework-related fights involve the problem of getting children to settle down and work, establishing and maintaining this homework routine will overcome many homework problems.

There are, however, children who will not willingly and easily comply with these routines, and they will need some firmer structures. Use the 'either/or' method described in Chapter 3 ('either you do your homework now, or you will not be allowed to watch any TV today'). Remember to stick to what you say. If homework is not done, then there must be no TV for your child – or whatever it is that you have said will or will not happen). You may also need to use behaviour modification as described in Chapter 1.

Another option for dealing with homework defiance is to use a process called 'natural consequences' (see Chapter 12, Discipline, for more details). Remember that setting up a place to do homework, and the routine itself, are initially your responsibilities. Doing the homework is your child's responsibility. If your child chooses not to do homework, there will be consequences at school. Don't protect your child from them, as facing the consequences of one's actions is another life skill. Be careful of falling into the trap that drags many parents into its grip – that of 'But what will they think of me as a parent?' So often, parents land up doing huge amounts of their children's work largely to protect their own reputation – that of being a good parent. This exhausts you and does not teach your child anything of value. In fact, by doing this, you teach your child to become learning-helpless, and they will forever be reliant on people to rescue them. They will also come to be the kind of person who blames everyone for their lack of competence.

Letting your child go to school with incomplete homework does not make you a bad parent. On the contrary, you will be helping your child learn to become responsible, develop independence and be able to face consequences. This is what good parents do. If your child refuses to complete their homework, simply sign the diary and make a note to the teacher saying that despite all efforts, your child would not do his or her homework and must face the consequences.

Handy hints

✍ In the beginning, just as with the other organisational structures described in this book, you will have to do some work. The choice of setting, desk, chair, lighting, waste paper bin and the organisation of stationery is your responsibility.

✍ Initially, stay at your child's side during homework time, especially when taking out books, stationery and deciding on the order in which to do the tasks.

✍ Do not set up the routine and then leave your child on his or her own too soon. You must help them stay with the homework routine for at least three weeks, until it becomes a habit. Stick to the times allocated on the weekly planner unless there is a crisis. The consistency and predictability of the time will help establish the routine.

✍ Use TV and playtime as rewards for completing homework on time. 'The quicker you get this done, the more time you'll have for …'

✍ Homework is not worth destroying the relationship between you and your child. If it really is causing unbearable tension, see if homework can be done at school or find a homework tutor (place an advert in the school newsletter or contact the Students' Union at your nearest university or college to find a good tutor).

✍ Bear in mind that children with learning difficulties will frequently battle with homework and may become quite defiant. If you have put all the structures in place as discussed in this chapter, but your child still struggles to complete the homework or works very slowly and needs lots of assistance, it is possible that they may have some form of learning difficulty. In this case you need to speak to your child's teacher and see what is happening at school. If the teacher reports problems at school too, then you may need to get professional assistance to address the learning difficulty.

8 Tackling tests and planning projects

> Your project is due when? Tomorrow?

> Why have you left all this for the last minute?

> I'm an eleventh-hour person. I work best under pressure.

> If you studied earlier, you would do better.

> I knew the answers but my mind went blank!

> For goodness sake, get yourself organised!

Eating the elephant one bite at a time

As if it isn't enough getting homework done without serious emotional damage, now along come all these tests and projects to stretch your nerves even further. Some tests are regular, like weekly spelling tests, which are prepared for in the daily homework slot. Then there are the 'elephants' – irregular tests and projects which can, if not adequately planned for, flatten you and your child emotionally and physically.

1. The 'elephants'

Schoolchildren are frequently given tests and projects to prepare for and present, but they are seldom given the 'tools' with which to tackle them. For most children, the prospect of preparing for a project or big test is similar to being asked to eat an elephant.

Because the idea of projects and tests can be overwhelming, they are frequently ignored for as long as possible in the hopes that the 'elephant' will go and bother someone else. Elephants, however, have a maddening ability to approach with surprising speed.

2. The dangers of close combat with 'elephants'

How often have you stayed up way into the night, desperately trying to tackle a project?

Many people are galvanised into action at the eleventh hour, and manage to produce excellent results. But it is an act of pure survival. During the eleventh hour your body kicks into 'fight-or-flight' mode, preparing to fight by secreting adrenalin. Riding this adrenalin tsunami, you attack the project and kill it before it kills you.

But what are the effects of this on your body? Exhaustion for a few days; headaches, nausea, heightened anxiety and restlessness as your body tries to re-balance its chemicals and do something with the inordinate amounts of adrenalin sloshing about, upsetting the liver and irritating the kidneys.

Not only does an 'all-nighter' flatten you physically, but don't you hate the little voice that niggles like a mosquito in your ear?

The elation of finishing the eleventh-hour sprint is quickly followed by self-doubt and chastisement, because you know full well that you are not an eleventh-hour person. You probably fiddled about, made one excuse after the other and had to work like mad at the last minute because you had left it all too late; not because doing so was a choice. Few people put themselves through hell by choice.

A final downfall of working at the eleventh hour is that you very seldom recall what you have actually done. Have you ever gone back to re-read a report, essay or exam paper a few months later, and felt as though it was not your own work?

These blanks are a common response to stress, and are due to the effects of adrenalin on the brain. Simply put, as soon as your brain senses danger, it prepares the body for fight or flight. The adrenalin prepares the big muscles in your body, such as those in your arms and legs, either to run very fast – or to fight back hard. It actually allows people to accomplish some spectacular feats (moms have been known to pick up cars that have trapped their children). However, things such as your digestive system shut down, as you do not have energy to waste on digesting food in a stressful situation. This is why children often complain of sore tummies on the day that they have to write tests. These are often *real* sore tummies, as their digestive systems are sluggish after not working properly the day before! Adrenalin also floods the brain in a stressful situation; since you often do not have time to think in such a predicament (Should I run away? Should I shout? Should I fight back? Should I just be still and quiet?).

No, in a stressful situation you simply react, on a more or less automatic level. There is often very little conscious, carefully considered decision-making taking place. This is all very well in a dangerous situation when your life is being threatened. However, if you have gone into fight-or-flight mode because you are scared that you are going to fail a test, then the fact that you cannot think clearly is not at all helpful.

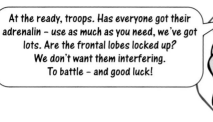

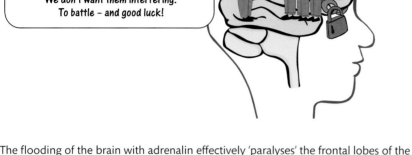

The flooding of the brain with adrenalin effectively 'paralyses' the frontal lobes of the brain, which is where we plan, organise, remember, think logically, make deductions, reason and generally do all of the brainy things that humans do. This temporary 'paralysis' is the reason for the dreaded exam 'blank'– that desperate feeling when you try to use your brain and it feels numb and useless.

Of course, as soon as the stress is reduced and the frontal lobes are given some room to work, the answers come flooding back, but much too late.

So, fighting with 'elephants' at the eleventh hour is dangerous on all levels. However, despite the dangers, we all do it over and over again? Why? Because no one ever taught us how to eat elephants – slowly and methodically, one bite at a time.

3. How to eat 'elephants'

TACKLING TESTS

Children need to learn to tackle tests in a systematic step-by-step manner. This means learning how to break the task of studying up into small, manageable portions and to get through these small portions daily, well in time for the due date. Not only does this help avoid stress and anxiety, it also prevents your child from studying in a 'parrot-fashion' manner which will ultimately make your child a real 'birdbrain'!

To understand how to tackle tests, imagine that your child has to study for a history test on the Early Inhabitants of South Africa. Let's be optimistic and assume that the due date is written on the homework sheet, the test is recorded on the monthly planner, and that your child knows what sections need to be studied.

What you do now is aim to complete a small portion of study every day, from the date the task is given to the day before the test. These small portions become part of the daily homework list, and shouldn't take more than ten to 15 minutes for younger children (possibly a little longer for older children).

STEP 1: GETTING THE BIG PICTURE

To begin with, all your child has to do is read through the work that will be covered in the test. Just read from beginning to end, without doing anything else (i.e. your child does not have to underline or write out the key words or summarise the work as he or she goes along). Just read. That's it; easy and do-able.

Going back to the example of the test on the Early Inhabitants in South Africa, all we want your child to be able to say after reading their work is, 'Hey, mom or dad, do you know that there were three different types of people living in South Africa before any white people arrived?' If your child can tell you that these people were called the San, the Khoi-Khoi and the Black farmers, then that is a bonus. Your child now has the big picture of what will be covered in the test. They have also had one repetition of the work (two, in fact, if they were listening carefully in class when these lessons were covered).

While reading through the work, your child is:

- Developing the 'big picture' of what has to be studied.
- Getting a sense of whether or not he or she actually understands the work.
- Seeing what notes and/or information is missing.

Once your child has finished reading through the work (and finished all the other homework), let him or her go and play. Studying is over for the day.

STEP 2: KEY WORDS

After having such an easy time on the first day of studying, your child should be quite enthusiastic to see what you have planned when you call him or her to study again the next day. Now you'll need coloured paper and coloured pens or pencils.

Choose one section from the work that will be covered in the test. This can be any section. It does not have to be the first section in the book. Let's say that your child chooses the Khoi-Khoi. He or she then has to read through this section and, on a piece of coloured paper, write down the key words. For something like the Early Inhabitants of South Africa, three different colours can be randomly assigned to each of the groups (for example, blue for the San, green for the Khoi-Khoi and red for the Black farmers). If your child is writing a science test on Energy, for instance, and the three sections covered in the test are heat energy, solar energy and water energy, then colour can be used quite specifically. Ask your child what colour they think heat energy is and if they say red, get them to write the key words on red paper. If they say the sun is yellow, then they write the key words for solar energy on yellow paper. The key words for water energy will be written on blue paper. Do not be prescriptive about the colours. If you think that the sun is yellow but your child says it is orange, let him or her write on orange paper. We are going to use colour to help cue the memory. For example, if a child is asked a question on water energy during the test, then he or she can think, 'Water? Water was on blue. What was written on my blue paper?' The child then tries to visualise what they wrote on the page. This is an additional tool to jog one's memory. It is useful to some, but not all, children. However, it is still worth using colour, for no other reason than that it is novel and interesting after always writing on white paper with a blue pen. The brain tends to respond well to things that are novel and interesting.

Identifying the key words is not always easy for children, as often they are not taught how to do this properly. What children tend to do is read one sentence of their work and write down the key words. Then they read the next sentence and write down the key words, and what they often end up doing is rewriting their notes, just without all the 'ands' and 'thes'. This is not a useful way of identifying key words. Instead, teach your child to read over a chunk of work, such as a paragraph. After they are finished reading, they must say what was important in the section. Teach them that there are usually only one or two important facts in a paragraph or section. The rest is all 'padding'. They need to learn to separate the facts from the 'padding', and only to write down the facts as key words. This prevents them from trying to learn the work in a 'parrot-fashion' (i.e. by rote, sentence by sentence, off by heart). What often happens when children learn 'parrot-fashion' is that they get stuck on one sentence that they just can't seem to memorise, and this blocks all the information that follows. By teaching children to identify the main facts and to learn only these, you reduce the amount of information that has to be memorised. The 'padding' usually also comes back to them when they think about the facts. If children learn just the main facts, they will always have enough information to pass their tests. The 'padding' is often what gets children the extra marks. But remember that this usually comes back to them if they remember the main facts, and also if they listen well in class.

Another tip is to encourage your child to use symbols and little pictures when doing key words. Many children today are visual learners, as a result of the invention of such things as television and the computer. Visual learners find pictures and symbols easier to remember than words made up of a group of abstract letters. Colour, pictures and symbols are useful cues to jog one's memory. An example is to encourage your child to draw a picture of a bow-and-arrow when discussing the San's weapons, or to draw an ostrich shell when describing their jewellery or the way in which they store their water.

RIGHT: Key words written on coloured paper

San
___

nomadic — moved around
lived in groups — 25-30 people
lived in caves
hunter gatherers
(men)   (women)
weapons — bow + arrows
         — spears
         — poison
stalked prey (disguises)
tracked prey for days
(could go without meat)
ate fruit, plants, seeds, roots, berries
ostrich eggs — to store water
            — jewellery
fire — rubbing sticks
clothes   men   women
         loincloth   leather aprons
                     jewellery
tools, weapons, clothing — from natural products
art — rock art   (hunts, special occasions, visitors)
    — dancing
    — oral stories

Once your child has finished reading through and writing down the key words for one section, he or she can once again go and play. If they have a lot of work to cover for their test, then they may have to do more than one section on day two, but remember not to leave them sitting at their desks for longer than 25 minutes without taking a break. Remember, we want them to work smart, not long.

While reading over a section and writing key words, your child is:

- Re-reading the information, so that he or she gets another repetition which is vital for learning.
- Thinking about what he or she is reading (not parroting or reciting).
- Identifying key words (the start of summarising).
- Working with colour, which is enticing to the brain and helps attention and memory.

STEP 3: KEY WORDS AND SENTENCES

On the third day your child takes the piece of paper containing the key words and, without looking in the book, uses each of the key words in a sentence. If they cannot remember what the key word means, they may look back in their book and jot down a few extra words to help them to remember. They can tell you the sentence orally or write it down on a piece of paper, but always remember to keep the colour of the paper the same for each section. If they wrote their key words for the Khoi-Khoi on green paper, then they must also write their sentences on green paper.

If your child has not been given much notice before the test, you can combine steps 2 and 3 and do both of these steps on one day. Let them write down the key words earlier in the day and later, after a break, they can come and tell you what each key word means to them.

While making up sentences using key words your child is:
*   Going over the work for the third time.
*   Repeating or re-writing the concepts and information in his or her own words and symbols, so that he or she is definitely not parroting or reciting.

It is a good idea to get your child to store their key words in the Study Guides section of the Ultimate Homework Diary so that they do not get lost.

Preceding days

Go through the same process for all the other sections to be covered in the test. Each section must be done on different-coloured paper. Remember, if possible to link the colour of the paper to the topic – for example, water energy on blue paper and solar energy on yellow or orange paper.

STEP 4: ONE-PAGE SUMMARIES

Once your child has gone through this process, he or she will have a number of different pages containing the key words from each section. The next step is to condense these pages onto one final summary page. This is where you start to make use of common summary techniques, including things such as mind maps, lists or tables. It is important to note that there isn't one 'best' method of summarising information. Mind maps seem to be a popular option, but they do not suit all children. They suit simultaneous (big picture) processors, but children who process information in a step-by-step, logical manner often struggle to learn from a mind map. To them it may look like a spider has spun a web on the page, and they are often not sure where to begin or how to follow the information trail. They usually prefer more structured summaries such as tables, lists or information written in neat boxes or columns.

It is important to be aware of the different summary options and to test out with your child which one they prefer the most. However, even if children love mind maps, it is also useful to teach them how to do tables, as this is the best method to summarise information that can be compared on a number of different variables. 'The Early Inhabitants of South Africa' is an ideal example of the kind of information that should be summarised in table form. The three different groups of inhabitants could be compared on some of the following variables: appearance, shelter, food, weapons, tools, etc. If this information is written up in table form, your child can easily see where these groups were similar, and what was different about each of them.

Let's look more closely at some examples of different summaries:

SUMMARY TECHNIQUE 1: MIND MAPS

Because your child already has all the key information written down, making a mind map at this stage should be very easy. Your child sits with their pages of key words and copies the information onto one page. The heading is put in the middle of the page, and has arrows radiating out from it for each of the sections that have to be learned. There is an example on the facing page.

It's good advice to keep the colour that your child writes the notes in for each section consistent with the colour of paper that they wrote their key words on. For example, if they wrote the key words for the San on blue paper, they must write their notes on the San in blue pen on their one-page summary. In this way the brain remembers that everything to do with the San was written in blue pen. This consistency may help to aid your child's recall of the information.

Remember to also encourage your child to use little symbols and pictures on the mind map.

SUMMARY TECHNIQUE 2: COLUMNS AND TABLES

Remember that this technique is often useful to a child who likes to work in a step-by-step, logical manner. The child takes a piece of paper and, instead of writing the heading in the middle of the page; he or she writes it at the top of the page where headings usually go. The page is then divided into as many columns as there are sections of work. In the case of the Early Inhabitants of South Africa, the page would be divided into three columns. The child then fills in the headings of each section. Colour is still important, and must be kept consistent (see page 94):

Early Inhabitants of South Africa

San	Khoi-Khoi	Black Farmers
Write key words in blue pen	*Write key words in green pen*	*Write key words in red pen*

The key words are then copied down in each column, once again remembering to make sure your child uses symbols and little pictures.

Columns can easily be converted into tables by adding an extra column in which your child writes the variable according to which the information can be compared. For example:

Early Inhabitants of South Africa

	San	Khoi-Khoi	Black Farmers
Appearance			
Shelter			
Food			
Weapons			
Tools			

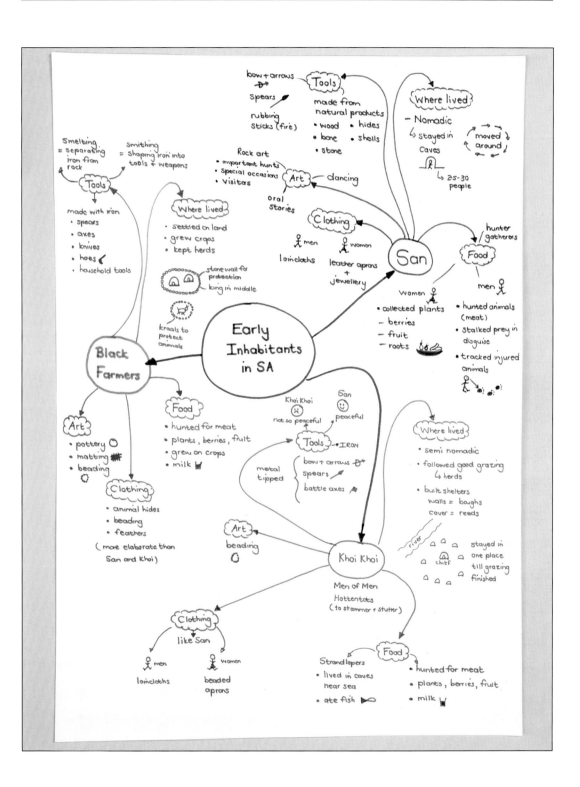

Early Inhabitants in SA

San

Tools
- bow + arrows
- Spears
- rubbing sticks (fire)

Tools
made from natural products
- wood
- bone
- stone
- hides
- shells

Where lived
- Nomadic
  - stayed in Caves
  - 25-30 people
- moved around

Art
Rock art
- important hunts
- Special occasions
- Visitors
- dancing
oral stories

Clothing
- men — loincloths
- women — leather aprons + jewellery

Food
hunter gatherers
Women
- collected plants
  - berries
  - fruit
  - roots
men
- hunted animals (meat)
- Stalked prey in disguise
- tracked injured animals

Black Farmers

Smelting = separating iron from rock
Smithing = Shaping iron into tools + weapons

Tools
made with iron
- spears
- axes
- knives
- hoes
- household tools

Where lived
- settled on land
- grew crops
- kept herds
- stone wall for protection — king in middle
- kraals to protect animals

Art
- pottery
- matting
- beading

Food
- hunted for meat
- plants, berries, fruit
- grew on crops
- milk

Clothing
- animal hides
- beading
- feathers
(more elaborate than San and Khoi)

Khoi Khoi
Men of Men
Hottentots
(to stammer + stutter)

Khoi Khoi — not so peaceful
San — peaceful

Tools — Iron
- bow + arrows
- spears
- battle axes
metal tipped

Where lived
- semi nomadic
- followed good grazing — herds
- built shelters
  walls = boughs
  cover = reeds
- stayed in one place till grazing finished
river / chief

Art
beading

Clothing
like San
- men — loincloths
- women — beaded aprons

Food
- hunted for meat
- plants, berries, fruit
- milk
Strandlopers
- lived in caves near sea
- ate fish

The information is then filled in on the table under the correct heading. Symbols and pictures can also still be used instead of actual words.

SUMMARY TECHNIQUE 3: LISTS

Some children have brains that work in a very linear fashion, and they would prefer to record their facts one underneath the other on their page. They then memorise these facts in order, and feel comfortable that they know their work. If this works for your child, then it is an acceptable way of summarising information. Colour, symbols and pictures can still be used in lists.

Early Inhabitants of South Africa

San *(everything relating to the San is written under this heading in blue)*
Khoi-Khoi *(everything relating to the Khoi-Khoi is written under this heading in green)*
Black Farmers *(everything relating to the Black Farmers is written under this heading in red)*

In each case, the key facts relating to each group are written in the appropriate colour beneath the relevant category. The colour-coding makes the facts easier to remember in the context of the group to which they apply.

As we've mentioned, one-page summaries should be quick and easy to make once your child has read over all their work and written down all the key facts. A great deal of the information should already be sticking in their brain, and they haven't even sat down to actually 'study' the work yet!

STEP 5: REVISING SUMMARIES

If you still have some days left before the test, your child can spend ten to 15 minutes each day revising their one-page summary. Remember – the more they repeat their work, the easier it will be for them to remember the information.

STEP 6: SETTING QUESTIONS ON THE WORK

Another useful step when studying is to ask your child to pretend that they are the teacher and to think of five questions that they would ask the children on this section of work. At first your child will probably come up with very simple questions. This is not a problem, but you could have a list of 'question words' available to help your child. Examples of 'question words' include:

What, why, where, when, how, who, do, does, compare, identify, describe, explain, list, name, etc.

After your child has thought of five questions themselves, you can also compile your own five questions on the work. If your child has straight-forward, simple questions, you can come up with slightly more difficult questions like those that teachers tend to ask.

Example: True or false:
         What is the difference between ...?
         In your opinion, ...

The questions are written on strips of paper or cardboard and can be used for a quiz on the night before the test. Better yet, play a game with these questions. For example you can play a board game like Snakes and Ladders or Ludo (and no; children do *not* outgrow these games – you yourself will be counting what you need to throw to go up the long ladder or to avoid coming down a snake!). Play the game as usual. Your child shakes the dice but, before he or she can move, a study question has to be answered. If your child gets the answer correct then they move the number of places shown on the dice. If they cannot answer the question, you provide the answer or you check back in the book and your child then misses their turn. It is then your chance and you also have to answer a question. Your child still learns, even while you are answering, as they have to listen to your answer to make sure that it is correct. Sometimes you can pretend not to know an answer (with the level of knowledge some children are getting at school, you probably won't have to pretend), and your child then has to give you the answer, thereby reinforcing his or her knowledge. Because you only have 10 questions, they come up again and again during the course of the game – which allows for effortless repetition of the work. After your child has answered the questions a number of times, and you can see that they really know the work, then put the questions aside and finish the game purely for the enjoyment of it and to see who wins.

By playing games with your child, you kill two birds with one stone. You get to check that your child knows their work, and you get to spend some fun time playing together. How many children do you know who spend the night before a test playing games? Your child will think you are 'the best' if you change your tactics and start to play more with him or her. We believe so strongly in the benefits of games as useful teaching tools that we will dedicate the whole of the next chapter to giving you some ideas on different games that can be used to improve your children's academic skills!

D-DAY

Your child 'aces' the test because he or she is confident, rested, knows the work well, and is not too anxious. Even better, though, the summary sheets and questions are filed for future use (preferably in the Ultimate Homework Diary), and when mid-year or final exams come around, you simply whip them out and revise.

Additional useful information regarding studying for tests

and memory techniques

(Adapted from a talk presented by Kevin Horsley)

Most children only use repetition as a means of improving their memory. They go over and over the work until they feel that they know it. The steps to studying as discussed above allow for lots of repetition, but there are some other useful pointers to remember in order to enhance your child's memory. These can be summarised by the word 'FLOOR', and hence we talk about the 'floor' approach to learning. Each letter in the word 'floor' stands for an important aspect of studying.

F   first things
L   last things
O   own links
O   outstanding information
R   repetition

FIRST AND LAST THINGS

We usually remember the things that we cover first when studying, because we are fresh and alert. We also remember the last things, as our brain often refocuses as we become excited because the end is in sight. This is why it is important to work for shorter periods and to come back and revise work. In this way we have lots of firsts and lasts. If children sit studying for long periods of time without a break, they have only one first and one last, and lots of information that gets forgotten in the middle.

OWN LINKS

Children need to understand information in order to be able to remember it. Meaning is vitally important to learning. Children also have a great deal of pre-existing knowledge that can be tapped into when studying. For example, if children are going to be taught about the tides of the ocean it is useful for them to have some idea of what an ocean is, and even better to have actually been to the beach before.

A child who has been to the beach will think, 'Ocean ... oh, yes, I have been to the ocean. I went to Durban in December. I remember mom said I couldn't swim at high tide because the sea was too rough!' This child will find it easier to learn about the tides of the ocean, because he or she has some previous experience of the topic. A child who has never actually been to the beach before will struggle to understand and learn about this topic. It would be exactly the same as trying to describe an elephant to someone who has never seen a real elephant, or even seen one in a picture or movie.

Of course, it is not always possible for someone to have had any experience of everything they will be taught. But, where possible, help your child to make links to their pre-existing knowledge. If this is not possible, then try and link the unknown information to something that your child does know well, such as their home.

Here is an example of how to do this. Let's imagine that your child has to learn 'The Timeline of Nelson Mandela'. Your child may have heard of Nelson Mandela, but does not know much about his life, so it will be difficult for him or her to link the new knowledge to any pre-existing knowledge. What you can do instead is ask your child to picture their home. Ask them what the first thing is that they see when they drive up to the house. It is usually a gate. Now tell your child to picture Mandela as a little baby in a crib at your gate. Link the information that he was born on July 18, 1918 in Umtata in the Transkei to this image. Next, tell your child to open the gate and look in the garden. There he or she must picture Mandela with some sheep and calves. As a young child, he was a herd boy. Then your child must picture the front door. Ask them what happens at the front door. You enter or leave the house. Mandela left home to go to Healdtown College in Fort Beaufort when he was 19 years old. Walk into the lounge. What do we do in the lounge? We have tea or drinks with people that we meet. Mandela met Winnie Mandela and, much later in life, Graca Machel. Ask your child to picture these two women sitting on different chairs. Then ask your child what happens when they are naughty. They get sent to their room for 'time out'. Mandela got sent to Robben Island for 'time out' in 1963. He was released 27 years later. And so on ...

In this way your child takes unknown information and links it to something familiar to them. In a test situation, they can think of the thing that is familiar to them and use this to help cue their memory. For example, 'My bedroom, my bedroom. What was in the bedroom? Oh yes, "time out". Mandela went for "time out" to Robben Island.' Other useful things to use when trying this technique are your car, your child's bicycle, and even the different parts of the body. All it takes is a little creativity.

OUTSTANDING INFORMATION

Things that are novel and interesting are the things that we remember. If someone is giving a speech and they put up a little cartoon or tell a joke, it is usually this that we remember. Then we stop and ask why they made use of the cartoon or joke, and this prompts us to recall what the speaker was trying to get across. It therefore makes sense that we should encourage our children to use novel and interesting things in their study notes to help them remember their work.

It is for this reason that things such as the use of colour and little pictures and symbols have been stressed in some of the previous sections.

These are all novel and interesting, and help to enhance memory. Other techniques include things such as mnemonics and rhymes. Mnemonics are when you take the first letter of each of your key words and make up a new word. For example, if you are learning the order of operations in mathematical sums, you learn the word 'BODMAS', which refers in letter order to Brackets, Of (e.g. 1/3 of 9), Division, Multiplication, Addition and finally Subtraction.

The word that your child makes up does not have to make any sense. For example, the name ROY G. BIV is a mnemonic for the colours of the rainbow (Red, Orange, Yellow, Green, Blue, Indigo, Violet). It merely has to contain the first letter of each of the key words. Some children love mnemonics, but others prefer rhymes. This is where they take the first letter of each key word and make up a little story. Again, it does not have to make sense. All children remember how to spell the word 'BECAUSE', thanks to the rhyme: 'Betty Eats Cakes And Uncle Sells Eggs'. If your child finds these techniques useful, encourage him or her to use them.

REPETITION

The more often you revise something, the better you will remember it. If you don't use it, you lose it! So use the FLOOR approach and as many other study tricks and techniques as possible, because the more cues you use, the better chance you have of pulling information out of your memory.

Preparing for projects, speeches and other assignments

When preparing for projects, speeches or other types of assignments, you use a similar technique – that of breaking the task up into small, manageable chunks. Let's imagine that your child has a project to complete on a wild animal.

Project instructions:
Choose a wild animal. Find out about its eating habits, where it lives and how it protects itself.
You also have to include a fully labelled picture of the animal.

When presented with this task, it may seem quite big and overwhelming to your child. What usually happens is that your child thinks, 'I have to decide on an animal, find some books or information about it, read the information, summarise it, write it out neatly and find pictures. Wow, that is too much. I think I will do it tomorrow.' Your child then avoids the project every day until there are no more 'tomorrows' – and then you and your child sit up until after midnight on the day before the project is due, trying to complete it. This, of course, does not happen without lots of shouting, fighting and tears. So how do you avoid this?

Firstly the project, speech or assignment needs to be noted on the Monthly Planner, so that it does not get forgotten. Then, remember the rule – anything on the Monthly Planner that involves work, has to be worked at for an agreed amount of time up to the due date. Your job as a parent is to teach your child how to take something as big and overwhelming as a project, speech or assignment and to break it down into smaller, manageable pieces. Going back to the example of a project on a wild animal, here is how you would do this:

STEP 1: BRAINSTORMING THE TOPIC

Tell your child to think about all the animals that they know, and to choose the one that interests them the most. If they say that they already know which one they want to do the project on, ask what it is and then tell them that their work for the day is over. They may now go and play. They have finished the first step of the project, which is deciding on the topic. The topic for this project is going to be elephants.

STEP 2: GATHERING INFORMATION

The next step is for your child to start gathering as much information on elephants as possible. They can start by looking for books and magazines that you have at home, or they could go to the school library at break or quickly after school. You could also schedule a day which would be convenient for you to go to the public library. It is a good idea to also note this down on the Monthly Planner, so that it isn't forgotten. You can't wait too long to go to the library, otherwise the project will be delayed.

If you have the internet at home, one evening can be scheduled to spend a little time obtaining information. Note that during this step you have just told your child to look for information. They do not have to read it or do anything else with it. All they are doing is gathering their resources for the project. This step may take more than a day or two, and includes buying any stationery that will be needed for the project.

STEP 3: DECIDING ON HOW TO PRESENT THE PROJECT

It is useful to decide on how the project will be presented before actually starting it, because then you will know how to plan the project. If the project is going to be presented in book format, then one section needs to be completed first, including pictures, before starting the next. If the project is going to be presented on cardboard, all the sections have to be completed before any can be stuck on the cardboard. Sometimes teachers tell the children how they want the project presented, in which case this step can be left out.

STEP 4: PLANNING AND KEY WORDS

This project on elephants has four different sections: What elephants eat, where they live, how they protect themselves, and a labelled picture. It is useful to help your child to sift through all the information that they have found in order to decide what is relevant to these four topics. For planning and organisation, it would be fantastic to have four different-coloured plastic envelopes and to sort the information and pictures into the envelopes. This could be the task for one day. On the next day, your child must choose the section that they would like to start with, and they then read through the information and write down the key words (as discussed earlier in this section). Each day your child could do a different section. The key words are then kept safely in the plastic envelopes, along with any pictures your child finds for the different sections.

STEP 5: EXPANDING ON KEY WORDS

Using the key words, your child can write up a rough draft or a paragraph on each section. Because you are not in a rush, there is time for editing, correcting and rewriting neatly. Depending on how much time is available and how much information they have, your child could write one or two sections neatly a day.

STEP 6: THE HEADING AND LAYOUT

This is the fun part your child has been waiting for – because all the hard work is over and it's time to lay out, decorate and illustrate the project.

STEP 7: HAND IN

If you work at this project one step at a time and a little bit each day, it should be finished on time. You will feel good because you will get to sleep the night before it is due, instead of staying up late to work. You will be able to drive your child to school with an immaculate project. (Don't leave it on the roof of the car by mistake!)

You will also feel proud – and possibly a bit weepy – because you will know how hard your child has worked, what effort it took on his or her part and how much he or she has learned, not only about elephants and what they eat, but how to eat elephants one bite at a time!

Handy hints

✎ Help your children plan for projects, but don't do the projects for them, because you will be depriving them of an unbelievably valuable learning experience.

✎ You will spend more time helping your child with the first few projects, but remember to spend the time teaching them how to do a project. In this way you will be able to withdraw from the process, and they will be able to do any future projects successfully on their own.

9 Fun 'n Games

> You played games at school? What am I paying for?

> Stop playing and come and do your work!

> My child doesn't take school seriously. All he wants to do is play!

> No, we are not playing games now. It's homework time.

> I hate spelling homework, hate it, hate it, hate it!

> All I ever do is nag and moan at my child. We never seem to have any fun together.

Learning to love learning

Anyone who tells you that playing games, for educational purposes or just for fun, is a waste of time is not in touch with good educational practice. It's simple, really. It's like the difference between spending an hour doing circuits at the gym, playing a great game of tennis, or hiking along a beautiful trail. All three will give you the exercise you need, but which are more motivating? Which will encourage you to get out of bed on a Sunday morning? The fun stuff, of course!

Why should you use games?

Games are like onions. They have layers and layers of benefits.

Games beat boredom

Games are a wonderful way to encourage your child to become involved in any type of learning that requires repetition – for example spelling, times tables, difficult or new reading words and even studying. A lot of this type of repetitive work can be incredibly boring (for you and your child) if done the wrong way. In fact, the boredom factor can become so high that it actually interferes with learning. Let's go back to the gym for a moment. You start off with enthusiasm and focus, but after a couple of days in the same environment, doing the same workouts on the same machines, are you still doing your best? Probably not. You are sweaty and bored and your mind starts to fantasise about all the other more fun things you could be doing. You lose focus on exercising properly and don't get the full benefit from the workout.

Games teach social skills

Playing games, from Hide and Seek to Snakes and Ladders, teaches children social skills such as following rules, taking turns, working in a group and winning or losing with grace. These are life skills that cannot be taught. They have to be learned in real-life situations.

Games have emotional benefits

Playing games also has emotional benefits. Very anxious children calm down when playing games, and children who struggle a little at school and who feel a bit different have a chance to experience success when playing games, which does wonders for their self esteem and confidence.

Games help build family bonds

Games are a wonderful way of improving family relations and strengthening bonds between parents and children. Many parents work hard and, what with running the home, homework, packing for the next day and all the other endless little jobs that eat up the day, there is often little time left to just have fun together. Games provide this time. If you manage to turn homework into a game, you not only get the boring work done in an enjoyable way, you also get the chance to have some fun time with your child.

Games develop foundation skills

Children are naturally programmed to play – not because they want to avoid work, but because it is through play that they develop all sorts of skills. Very physical games that involve running, climbing, throwing and catching develop muscle strength and tone. Building games like Lego and blocks develop visual perceptual skills (making sense of what you see), fine motor skills, planning and organisation. A board game like Cluedo and the card game Go Fish help develop, amongst other things, auditory perceptual skills (making sense of what you hear). Other card games are also excellent for developing visual perceptual and mathematical skills. These foundation skills must be in place before children start school, or there is a chance that they may struggle to develop good reading and writing skills.

FIT FOR SCHOOL

Games and homework

As you are well aware, homework can be a nightmare. If, however, you make use of games, homework can become not only bearable, but positively enjoyable for you and your child! You are probably rolling your eyes at this, but it's true. You just need to learn how.

How to have fun with spelling

Of all the homework tasks, spelling seems to create the most chaos. Spelling is hard, it needs a lot of repetition, it is boring and for children who struggle to spell, it is a really tedious, unfulfilling task. But it has to be done.

The scenario

Your child comes home on Monday with the dreaded spelling words that need to be learned for the inevitable test on Friday. You immediately get a headache, knowing in advance the problems that this is going to create in your home because your child (along with tens of thousands of other children) hates spelling with a vengeance.

A. WHAT DO YOU USUALLY DO?

You nag, yell and threaten your child into sitting at the homework desk. You strap him or her down so they can't escape and go through the time-honoured, mind-numbing routine of looking at the word, covering the word, writing the word, and checking the word. To make matters worse, your child is equipped only with a piece of white paper and a lead pencil, both of which have all the allure of a dead rat. After half an hour both of you are wondering what you must have done in the past to deserve this torture.

To top it all off, after four days of dedicated torture your youngster only gets five words right in the spelling test, and the dictation is a disaster!

B. WHAT SHOULD YOU DO?

You can re-invigorate this whole process and make it useful and fun (as well as add years to your life) by turning spelling into a game. This is easy, cheap, and the rewards are surprising, both from an academic and emotional point of view. Amazingly enough, spelling can become an activity that draws you closer to your child instead of being the wedge that splits you apart.

Making spelling special

1. ON YOUR MARKS

You will need scrap paper and/or cardboard (both white and coloured paper – ask the stationer for a 'memo cube refill'); some board games (Snakes and Ladders and Ludo are a good start, and cheap to buy); coloured pens or pencils and possibly a stopwatch (for the matching game).

2. GET SET

Make two packs of blank cards, preferably on two different colours of paper. The cards can be about half the size of a regular playing card. The easiest way to make these cards is to take a piece of small, square notepaper and fold it in half. This is the perfect size and, because the paper is folded, it is thick enough so that the children won't be able to see the words through the page, which is important for some of the games. If time allows, get your child to fold the paper, as this allows for some fine motor practice as well as learning spelling. Each pack must contain as many cards as there are spelling words that need to be learned. If you have 15 spelling words, then each pack will have 15 cards.

Once the cards have been folded (or cut out, depending on what paper you are using), get your child to write each of the spelling words on the cards. Depending on which game you are going to play, they may only need to make one set of cards today and another later in the week – or they may have to make both sets of words at the same time. What you will end up with is two identical packs of words. In this way, they get two opportunities to practice writing their spelling words. There is also far more motivation to write the words because, when they ask you why they must do it, you can tell them that it is so they can play a game. This is far more motivating than writing the words out over and over again in their books simply because they have to.

It is very important that you check all the cards carefully to make sure that the words are spelled correctly before you start to play any games with your child. They are going to see the words that they have written on the cards over and over again, and so it is important that there are no errors, or these will be imprinted on your child's brain. If there are cards with mistakes, it is better to throw these away and to make new cards rather than erasing the mistake, because even when you erase words there is often a negative imprint which the brain will continue to see.

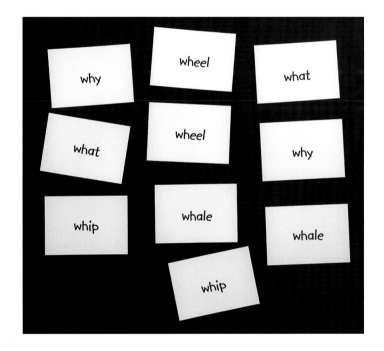

These cards will be called the 'working cards', because they are going to be used in a whole lot of different ways for the rest of the week to help your child learn how to spell their words.

3. GO!

Use these working cards daily in different games. You can play the same game for a whole week, if that is what your child wants to do (Bingo often has them hooked for a long time), or you can choose a new game every day to add spice to your child's spelling.

Please note that your child does not have to write their words out over and over again to learn how to spell them. The more times that they see the words spelled correctly, the better they will imprint on their brain. This improves their visual memory for words.

Game A: Bingo

BASIC PREPARATION FOR 2 OR MORE PLAYERS

- One set of working cards.
- Counters or small coins (beans and raisins also make good counters).
- Coloured pens or pencils.
- 2 sheets of A4 paper divided into grids of 9 (for young children) or 16 blocks. You will need more paper if more players are playing. These are the Bingo boards.
- Each player writes the spelling words onto their Bingo board, making sure the words are in different places on each board. (In this way your child gets another chance to practice writing their spelling words. If they will, ask them to help you by filling in your Bingo board, which will give them one extra practice. If they are not keen, don't force the issue. Just quickly fill in the words yourself.)

NOTE:

If your child does not have 16 words to learn for the week, add some of last week's words for further consolidation or add in words that you know that your child struggles to spell. Remember that you will have to put these words onto the working cards as well.

TO PLAY

1. One person is the caller. They have the working cards.
2. This person can call out the words in a number of different ways. They can hold up the card for everyone to see and read the word; in this way the word goes into your child's brain through both the visual and auditory channels. The caller may just hold up the word, and everyone has to look and read it for themselves. In this way you are only using the visual channel. The caller may also look at the word and read it without showing anyone else. In this way your child has to listen and then find the word. The information goes in through the auditory channel. A number of different channels of learning can, therefore, be accessed with this game.
3. After seeing or hearing the word, all the players look for it on their boards and cover it with a counter.
4. The game is not won simply when someone has covered all their words, because everyone has the same words – so everyone would win at the same time. Instead, play continues until someone has covered either three (on the 9-block grid) or four (on the 16-block grid) words in a row. This can be from top-to-bottom, left-to-right or diagonally.
5. Once someone gets three or four in a row they shout 'BINGO!', and the game is won.
6. This game is quick and easy, and children usually want to play again and again and again. So play again. It is so much fun and an effortless way of repeating their words!

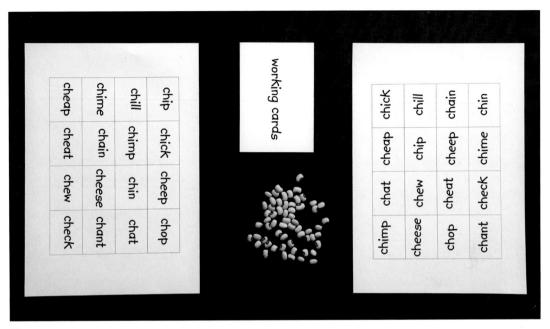

Bingo

Game B: Speedy Gonzales (Matching Game)

BASIC PREPARATION FOR ONE PLAYER
- Use one of the Bingo boards and one pack of working cards.
- A stopwatch.

TO PLAY
1. Your child has to place each of the working cards over the matching word on the Bingo board as fast as he or she possibly can.
2. Do this at least twice on one board, and then change to the other board.
3. Time each round, using a stopwatch to see which is the fastest round.
4. You can do this as a competition between two players. Each player has a board, and they race each other to see who can cover all the words first.

Game C: Snap

BASIC PREPARATION FOR TWO PLAYERS
- Both sets of working cards.

TO PLAY

1. Each player holds a set of well-shuffled working cards face down.
2. On the count of three, each player turns over the top card and places it on the table.
3. If the words are the same, this is SNAP – and the player who calls first wins the cards.
4. The player who collects the most cards wins.

NOTE:

If you are sitting opposite your child when playing this game, it is important that you put your cards upside down, allowing your child to read both the words the same way. You will have to read both the words upside down – but because this is a visual matching game, we want your child to see both the words the same way up and not one the right way up and the other upside down.

If you find this difficult, sit next to your child and you can both place the cards the same way up, but next to each other on the table.

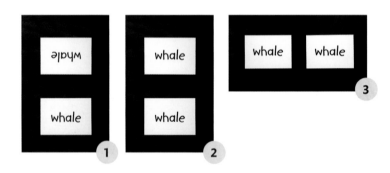

SNAP CARDS: Example 1 is incorrect, whereas examples 2 and 3 are correct

Game D: Memory Matching (Pick up Pairs)

BASIC PREPARATION FOR TWO OR MORE PLAYERS

- Both sets of working cards.
- Each set is laid down in a neat grid pattern on a table.

TO PLAY:

1. The aim is to pick up two identical words, one from each set of the working cards (this game is more difficult if the two sets of words are written on the same coloured paper).
2. Player 1 picks up one card from each set (or any two cards if the words are on the same colour paper). He or she has to read the words.

3. If the words are the same, the player holds onto the pair. If they are different, they must be put back in the same place.
4. Player 2 then picks up two words.
5. Players take turns until there are no more cards on the table. The player with the most pairs wins.

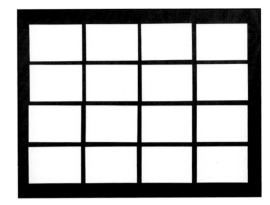

RIGHT: Placement of cards for Memory Matching

Game E: Board Games (e.g. Snakes and Ladders and Ludo)

BASIC PREPARATION FOR TWO OR MORE PLAYERS
*   One pack of working cards.
*   A board game.
*   Counters and dice.

TO PLAY
1. Place one pack of working cards face down next to the board.
2. Play the game as normal. The first player shakes the dice, but before they can move, another player turns over a card and reads it. The first player then has to spell the word.
3. Check the spelling. If it is correct, the player can move forward the number of spaces shown on the dice. If the word is incorrect, they must look carefully at the card and spell the word again whilst looking at it. The card is then placed at the bottom of the pile and the person misses their turn (i.e. they are not allowed to move).
4. Play continues in this way, with each player having a chance to spell the words. Even when your child is not actually spelling the word, he or she is learning. They have to listen carefully, or check the working card while someone else spells a word to ensure that it is correct. So even when it is your turn, your child is learning.
5. Continue until someone wins the game.
6. This game is excellent for effortless repetition, because your child will be so focused on winning the game that he or she will forget that they are doing spelling. You, of course, are focused on the spelling words, but will also have fun playing the game. If the game goes on for a while, the words will come up time and time again, which is great for repetition. However, if you can see that your child knows the words well and is getting bored, then put them aside and finish the game just for the fun of playing, and to see who wins. But before you do this, have one round where everyone has to make a sentence with the words. You do this to make sure that your child knows what the word means. It is pretty pointless learning how to spell a word if you do not know what it means.

4. The finish line

In going through the process of making and playing the different games, your child will experience a huge amount of repetition in an effortless, imaginative way which will stimulate motivation and result in real learning.

What can I remember?

To consolidate and strengthen the spelling learned while playing the games, keep a record of the words your child can remember and write correctly. Divide a piece of paper into four columns (one for each of the days of the week leading up to the Friday test). Head the page, 'Measuring my Memory'. After each game, challenge your child to write down as many words as he or she can remember. Every day your child will be able to remember – and spell – more and more words.

Useful Tips:

- If you have an older child who no longer gets regular lists of words to learn, or you just want to improve your child's spelling, there are useful lists of words available to help improve your child's sight-word pool. These include the lists of trick words, the hundred most often misspelled words and the Dolch sight-word list. Teachers and remedial therapists often have copies of these lists. Choose a few words from these lists and play the above games with your child in the evenings instead of watching television, and watch their spelling skills improve dramatically.
- If you want your child to get more practice actually writing out his or her spelling words, then make sure that you make this as novel and fun as possible. Remember that things that are novel and interesting appeal to the brain and help to keep children motivated. It is, therefore, important to introduce lots of colour and different mediums to enhance your child's learning. Stock up with many different-coloured pens, pencils, felt-tipped pens, wax crayons, chalk and magnetic letters, and get your child to write on various surfaces such as:

  - Coloured paper.
  - Blackboards.
  - Whiteboards.
  - The fridge (using magnetic letters or non-permanent pens).
  - The bath (with bath crayons).
  - Flour or salt (in a Tupperware container).
  - Sand (in a sandpit or in a Tupperware container)
  - Velvet material (they can scratch on this with their finger).
  - Their own bodies (especially on their arms or backs).

The end result will be children who are not only learning, but having fun while doing so and building their self-confidence and self-esteem at the same time.

Other uses for the working cards

The working cards do not only have to be used to improve spelling skills. They can also be used to practise a number of other skills, for example:

READING NEW OR TRICKY WORDS
Have two identical packs of working cards and use as for spelling. Each time your child plays a game, they merely have to read the words.

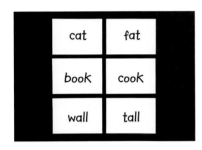

RHYMING WORDS
- These packs work extremely well for Snap and Memory Matching (Pick-up pairs).
- For Bingo, call the word from one pack – 'cat', for example – and your child has to cover the rhyming word on the Bingo board, which is 'fat'.
- For Snakes and Ladders, read the word from one pack and encourage your child to give you any rhyming word.

OTHER LANGUAGE SKILLS
You can drill any language skill using the games above. Some ideas include antonyms (opposites), synonyms (words with the same or similar meanings), homonyms (words with the same sound or spelling but different meanings), similes (comparisons of one thing with another as an illustration; for example 'as brave as a lion'), plurals and tenses. You can also drill the different parts of speech such as nouns, verbs, adjectives and adverbs. If playing Snap, you say 'snap' if two nouns come up, for example. The words are now no longer the same, and your child really has to think and concentrate in order to win. When playing Memory Matching, you have to pick up two words that are the same part of speech; or two antonyms or two synonyms and so on. Board games can also be used to drill language skills. Your child turns over the card and, before moving, has to tell you what part of speech the word is or give you the antonym or synonym of the word.

Examples of things to include on the working cards:

PARTS OF SPEECH:	**Pack 1:** house	**Pack 2:** common noun
PLURALS:	**Pack 1:** pen	**Pack 2:** pens
TENSES:	**Pack 1:** walk	**Pack 2:** walked
ANTONYMS:	**Pack 1**: fat	**Pack 2:** thin
SYNONYMS:	**Pack 1:** thin	**Pack 2:** slender
HOMONYMS:	**Pack 1:** horse	**Pack 2:** hoarse
SIMILES:	**Pack 1:** white	**Pack 2:** snow

STUDY QUESTIONS:
See Chapter 8 – Tackling Tests and Planning Projects.

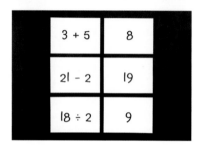

TRANSLATIONS

The same games can be used to help children learn their second language. All you need is one set of working cards in English, and the other set with the words translated into the second language. Now play all the above games with these two sets of cards.

MATHEMATICAL CALCULATIONS

- Snap and Memory Matching are played as normal, but you 'snap' or match the sum to the answer.
- For Bingo, write either the sums or the answers to the sums on the grids. Call, for example a sum like 11 – 2, and your child covers the answer.
- For Snakes and Ladders, shuffle both sets of working cards. When you pick up a card, your child will either have to give an answer to a sum (5 x 3) or a sum for an answer (15).

IN THE SAME WAY YOU CAN WORK WITH:

FORMULAS:	Pack 1:	AREA	Pack 2:	Length x breadth
DEFINITIONS:	Pack 1:	triangle	Pack 2:	Shape with three sides.
TIMES TABLES:	Pack1:	1 x 6	Pack 2:	6

Other ideas for Maths

DICE

- Use two or three dice.
- Throw the dice and add the numbers on the face of the dice.
- Use two dice to practise times tables and subtraction.
- The person who gets the answer first is the winner.

You can also drill the concepts 'biggest', 'smallest'and 'same as' using dice.
- With two players, you need two dice.
- Each player shakes their die and throws it on the table. You have to decide beforehand which concept you are drilling (e.g. biggest).
- The first person to pick up the die with the biggest number on it gets a point.
- The first person who reaches 10 wins the game.

- Players get minus points if they pick up the wrong die or if they pick up a die when both have the same number (this is the 'same as'). This helps to curb impulsivity.
- After playing first one to pick up the 'biggest' number, change and play first to pick up the 'smallest' one.
- Once your child is good at this, change and get someone to call 'biggest' or 'smallest' every time just before you throw the dice. This makes your child listen carefully and is good exercise for the brain, because it has to keep changing between concepts, which improves cognitive flexibility.

Not only does this game improve mathematical skills, it also improves eye movements, as the eyes have to look across the table continually to see the dice, wherever they land. Added to this, it improves fine motor skills as children pick up the small dice.

PLAYING CARDS
- A cheap pack of playing cards is a great learning tool. Either play games like Rummy, Go Fish or Patience, or use the pack of cards to play *Snap* and *Memory Matching*.
- You can also use them to practise calculations. Shuffle the pack and deal ten cards to each player. These cards are held in a pack, face down. On the count of three, each player flips the top card and places it on the table. Players have to add, subtract or times (multiply) the numbers featured on the cards. The first person to come up with the answer wins the cards. The winner is the person with the most cards at the end of the game.
- You can also drill the concepts 'biggest', 'smallest' and 'same as', using cards as you do with dice – but, instead of picking up the cards, the winner is the first one to place their hand on the correct card.

Please note: Most of the games covered in this chapter are visual games. Don't forget also to play auditory games with your child such as 'Eye Spy ...', 'Go Fish' and 'I went to the shop and bought ...'.

Handy hints

✎ Encourage your children to make the games themselves. The games do not have to be neat and pretty; they only have to work.

✎ Laminate blank bingo grids and card packs. Write on them with non-permanent markers. Wipe clean each week, ready for new words.

✎ Don't always let your child win. Life involves both winning and losing, and your child must learn how to cope with both outcomes.

✎ Have as much fun as possible.

10 Handling the TV menace

> My child loves the Discovery channel. He will spend hours and hours watching.

> Why are all these children in therapy?

> Isn't it amazing what three-year-olds can do with a computer these days!

> My child never listens. I may as well speak to the wall!

> I can't get my child to switch off the TV set. He's glued to the thing.

> Computer games are great for hand-eye co-ordination. I let my child play all the time!

'The greatest unacknowledged health scandal of our time'

Dr A. Sigman, Associate member of the British Psychological Society

What is your child doing while you are reading this chapter? Doing homework? Hopefully – but unlikely. Playing outside? Maybe. Watching something on a screen? Probably! If your child is watching TV, a DVD or playing a computer game, you are probably sighing with relief – because you know that your child is safe and not getting up to mischief. This means you can get a few blessed minutes of peace and quiet.

The question is, just how safe *is* your child in front of that screen? What's happening – or rather, what *isn't* happening in the hours that your child spends glued to the box?

There is no doubt that the technological age benefits us in many ways. But children who are placed in the path of the technological tidal wave without any buffering can be profoundly affected and suffer some potentially serious, long-term effects on their development.

The terrors of television

The most prominent of the technological menaces is television. For many families the TV has almost become a member of the family; the babysitter, the entertainer, the stress-reliever and the consoler. Television has insidiously intruded itself into our lives, and quietly exerts powerful influences over us. We're blissfully unaware of many of them.

What the research says

Much TV-related research has been published by the likes of *The Journal of Pediatric and Adolescent Medicine*, John Hopkins School of Public Health, Stanford University, The Department of Pediatrics (Rhode Island Hospital), Yale-New Haven Children's Hospital, the American Academy of Pediatrics, the *Biologist Journal*, *The US Pediatrics Journal*, the Albert Einstein College of Medicine (N.Y.), the American Optometric Association and the British Association of Behavioural Optometrists.

The result of this research is conclusive. Watching excessive television can be very damaging to children. 'Phew,' you think, 'that's not my child. They must have researched those American children who watch an average of five to six hours of television a day.' Think again. All of the research suggests that even two to three hours a day is excessive. The research also says that children below the age of two should not be exposed to television at all.

Watching excessive amounts of television has negative effects on:
- Physical development.
- Maintaining appropriate weight.
- Physical health.
- Sleep patterns.
- Eyesight and eye movement development.
- Listening skills.
- Language development.
- Attention and concentration.
- School performance and homework.
- Social interactions.

In short, watching too much television can negatively affect virtually every aspect of your child's development. Let's look at some of these in a little more detail to raise your awareness.

Physical development

The next time you are watching television, have a careful look at your child. Chances are he or she resembles a somewhat empty, shapeless potato, slouched across the couch.

There is no movement, except perhaps the odd limb reaching out to grab another snack. This is so sad, because while your child is sprawled on the couch in front of the television, he or she is losing out on hours and hours of exercise and playtime which are absolutely critical, not only for physical development, but also for brain development and learning. Many leaders in the field of learning such as Howard Gardner, Jean Ayres, Rudolf Steiner and Maria Montessori have stressed the importance of movement in the learning process. Every time we move, especially in an organised manner, brain activation and integration occurs and we open the door to learning. The more we limit our children's movement by allowing them to sit still for hours in front of the TV, or by forcing them to sit still and learn at a desk, the more difficult it will become for them to actually learn.

Children's bodies must move in order to develop. This means they must be running around, swinging, playing sport and generally spending time getting sweaty and red in the cheeks every day.

From a physical point of view, a lack of movement may result in difficulties with your child's bone density, core muscle strength, muscle tone, balance and co-ordination. These are developed and strengthened naturally through play and movement.

WHAT DO YOU SEE AT SCHOOL?
School is very demanding on little bodies. Just sitting upright at a desk for a few hours each day takes a lot of strength and energy. Children with low muscle tone, limited muscle strength, and poor balance and co-ordination tend to struggle physically to get through the day.

They tire easily, and often complain of a sore neck and shoulders. Their concentration is also affected, because they are physically tired and uncomfortable, and they tend to give up very easily on tasks that require perseverance. Added to this, their work is often described as slow, untidy, poorly planned and disorganised. You will read comments in their books such as, 'Matthew is not working to his full potential', or 'This is all John managed to complete in an hour's lesson' or 'Portia is a clever child, but she needs to get organised'. Their poor physical development has an impact on every aspect of their learning.

Weight

Added to poor physical development, sitting and watching too much television contributes to weight gain. Obviously children who don't move enough do not burn up calories, and thus they gain weight. Combined with the lack of movement, watching television tends to be accompanied by snacking on fattening junk foods.

Carrying too much extra weight has major health risks. Currently there is global concern about childhood obesity and the high incidence of early-onset Type 2 diabetes in children. Some experts are even calling it an epidemic. This early-onset Type 2 diabetes is being linked to poor eating habits and a sedentary lifestyle. The long-term effects of diabetes, other than the constant constraints of medication and diet, are blindness, kidney failure and limb amputations due to poor circulation.

WHAT DO YOU SEE AT SCHOOL?
While being overweight is a health hazard, it also carries with it social and emotional difficulties. Overweight children are often ostracised by their peers, ignored, teased and bullied. They also struggle to perform well at sports, and are often not chosen for teams. Their lives can, therefore, be fraught with social failures that could lead to other problems such as depression or eating disorders.

Sleep patterns

Children should have at least eight solid hours of sleep a night to give their bodies and brains time to regenerate in order to be able to cope with the demands of each new day. Watching as little as two hours of television a day can prevent children from getting enough deep, sound sleep. One reason for this is that we are biologically programmed to produce higher levels of the hormone melatonin as daylight fades and evening sets in. Melatonin is one of the hormones that quietens the body and helps it prepare for sleep. Watching television and staring at the bright flickering screen reduces melatonin, and affects the body's natural waking and sleeping rhythms.

Low levels of melatonin affect a child's ability to fall asleep easily. This situation can lead to difficult bedtimes. Your child may put up a fight about going to bed, which will interfere with the smooth running of your evening routine. Otherwise your child may have trouble falling asleep, may not sleep for long enough, or may be restless during the night.

   Watching too much television not only interferes with the body's chemical transition into sleep mode, but if your child is glued to the TV for long periods during the day, he or she will also miss out on all the physical activities, which wear him or her out and promote sleep.

The result of watching too much television is a combination of too little melatonin and too much unused energy, which is a deadly combination for healthy sleep.

Of course, if your child is not sleeping well, there is a good chance that you are not either. Lack of sleep often has a significant impact on a person's mood, and so you may find your whole family irritable and tired in the mornings when you are trying to institute an efficient morning routine. Tempers often flare and everyone leaves home in a bad mood, which does not set a good tone for the rest of the day.

WHAT DO YOU SEE AT SCHOOL?
A lack of sleep has a significant impact on a person's ability to sustain their attention over time. If you can't concentrate, you can't learn.

Eyesight and eye movement development

Roll your eyes around. Now sweep them from left to right and back again. Move your head from left to right. Now keep your head still and move only your eyes from left to right. Look up from this page and into the distance and then look back at the page again. You have just given your eyes a workout. This does not happen when you sit glued to the television as, your eyes fix at one distance. Actually, when our eyes stop moving, as when staring at a television screen, visual input also stops. Have you ever noticed that when you stare at something, you miss what is happening in your environment?

Every movement that your eyes make is due to tiny muscles which, like all other muscles, need movement to develop appropriately. For eye muscles to develop optimally, children must be involved in the three-dimensional world. They need to play games and sports that make their eyes focus on distant and close objects, objects in the centre of their vision, objects to their left and right, objects above and below them and objects that roll and bounce. Staring at a flat, two-dimensional television screen which does not move and does not force the eyes to move, will not provide your child with enough eye exercise.

Just like every other muscle in our bodies, if we don't exercise our eye muscles, they become weak. This then results in difficulty with eye tracking (the smooth movement of both eyes working together) and convergence (ability to focus near and far). More and more children are being sent to optometrists and are being diagnosed, not with poor eyesight, but with 'lazy' eyes. If your child's eyes can't track smoothly, he or she will struggle to read. If your child has convergence difficulties, he or she will struggle to copy work accurately from the board as he or she will struggle to change focus from far (the board) to close up (their book).

WHAT DO YOU SEE AT SCHOOL?
Simply put, a child who cannot see well and whose eye muscles tire easily will not learn well.

Listening skills

As you may have noticed, children appear to have lost the ability to listen properly. Why? Being able to listen is a learned skill, which needs to be developed through practice. This practice involves having good old-fashioned conversations with your child, where you both get to listen and speak. Now you may be thinking: 'But I speak to my child all the time, and he or she still ignores me!'

In our hectic schedules, there is little time to really talk and communicate with our children. All we seem to manage is to bark out orders and rules. We speak at children, but not with them and, sadly, we seldom really take the time to listen to what they say.

Now add television into this already problematic situation, and your child's chances of developing listening skills are blown to pieces. You may be thinking, 'But hold on – the characters speak, so surely my child can learn from listening to them?' This is not true. Most children watch television and absorb what they are seeing through their eyes. They do not really listen to the dialogue. If you ask them what they have been watching, they will often describe what they have seen and not what they have heard.

Even if your child does actually listen to the dialogue, he or she still does not have to respond to or participate in the conversation. He or she, therefore, does not learn about the social aspects of speaking to people – such as turn-taking, and listening to and answering questions meaningfully. These skills are only developed through real-life communication with real people. Barney may be educational, but he will never be able to teach your child how to have a conversation.

So, the next time you ask your child a question and all you get in return is a shrug, a grunt or nothing at all, don't 'lose it' and start shouting. Stop, breathe and remember that children brought up on too much television from an early age will not listen to you – not because they are disrespectful, ungrateful and selfish, but because they don't know how.

WHAT DO WE SEE AT SCHOOL?

Listening is critical for learning. Children who have not developed good listening skills (which should be developed well before the start of Grade R, so don't blame the teacher) often struggle to understand what the teacher is saying. They also battle to follow instructions and become difficult from a behavioural point of view because they get confused about what to do. Children who have poor listening skills also tend to 'tune out' and stop paying attention, because they are overwhelmed by the amount of listening that has to be done.

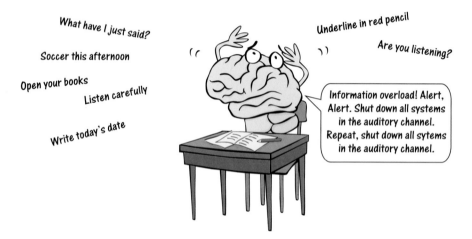

Children who 'tune out' as a survival strategy in class are often thought to have an Attention Deficit Disorder – but, when this is treated as such, they do not show significant improvement.

Language development

Language development is linked to listening. The development of language – in this case speaking, vocabulary and general knowledge – is not always improved by watching television. Television programmes usually rely on good visual effects to keep children hooked, and not on good language. In fact, sometimes children can learn quite inappropriate language from TV. They are also often confused by people's responses to what they say when they repeat what they heard because, on the TV, everyone laughed – but here you are, shouting at them. 'Ah, I've got you there,' you think. 'My child only watches documentaries, which are very educational.' Yes, they are, but only if you are sitting with your child, explaining what they are seeing.

Little children do not have the ability to understand adult documentaries on their own. Again, they will watch the pictures and not listen to the information unless you are there to help.

WHAT DO WE SEE AT SCHOOL?

Children with poorly-developed language skills struggle to express themselves clearly. Children with limited vocabulary and general knowledge often struggle with comprehension tasks. Also, listening and speaking are the foundations for reading and writing. So a child who struggles to listen and speak has a strong chance of struggling to read and write.

Every hour watched, is an hour lost!

You now know about the dangers of television, and hopefully you have been persuaded to limit the time that your child spends in front of the 'tube'. Remember that television in itself is not *bad*. Rather, it is the amount of *time* that your child spends in front of the television in one sitting that is problematic. Let your child choose one programme to watch, and encourage them afterwards to go outside and play. They can then come back to the television later in the day to watch some more.

Handy hints

✍ Switch off the TV and play games instead. This will benefit your whole family, not just your child.

✍ Under no circumstances should your child have a television in the bedroom. If you give them one, then you can expect trouble. Apart from making your child anti-social and isolating them from the family, it is very difficult to control what they are watching in their own rooms. Be careful of falling into the parent peer-pressure trap of trying to compete and outdo other parents. If someone boasts about having a television in every room of their house, just smile pityingly and say 'shame'.

- If your child is at a nursery school where television is used to 'babysit' children in the afternoon, have a serious chat to the principal. These children should be outside playing and squelching mud between their toes.

- Do not have the television on in the morning while you are rushing around to get ready. Cartoons will outdo getting ready for school every time.

- Use television as a treat, for example, 'If you finish your homework on time, then you can watch an extra ten minutes of TV.'

- Choose the programmes your child watches with care. In between the sitcom nonsense and bloodbath thrillers are some great shows, and wonderful films that are a treat to watch.

- Treat television like a slab of chocolate. Instead of eating the whole thing in one go, which makes you feel sick and adds to your hips, rather parcel it out in small delicious bites that you can savour and enjoy, guilt-free.

11 Feed your body, feed your brain

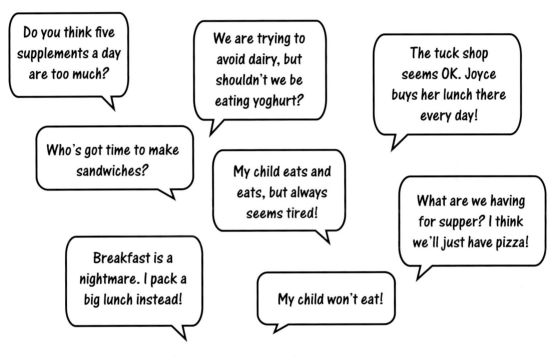

Do you think five supplements a day are too much?

We are trying to avoid dairy, but shouldn't we be eating yoghurt?

The tuck shop seems OK. Joyce buys her lunch there every day!

Who's got time to make sandwiches?

My child eats and eats, but always seems tired!

What are we having for supper? I think we'll just have pizza!

Breakfast is a nightmare. I pack a big lunch instead!

My child won't eat!

Eating for optimal brain power

Knowing what foods to eat is confusing for many people. Butter or margarine? Wholewheat or multigrain? Low fat or fat-free? Sugar-free? Yes? No? Carbohydrates or proteins? The confusions are many and overwhelming. One week you are avoiding meat; the next you are worried about iron deficiencies. Then milk becomes the monster, but – on the other hand – yoghurt is good for you. It is enough to make you want to throw your arms up in despair and buy a cheeseburger from the nearest take-away. Fortunately there is a way to minimise the confusion and keep some focus on what you should be feeding your child.

The main components of the brain

Think of your car. What do you need to put in your car's engine to keep it from seizing up and coming to a steamy halt? Water, oil and good-quality petrol. On top of this, you also need to look after your car's bodywork, to ensure that it does not fall apart. Well, brains are like cars – they also need regular top-ups of water, oil and 'petrol', and they need their bodywork maintained. The three biggest components of your brain are water, essential fatty acids and proteins, and the more brain food you feed your brain, the better it works.

The water your car needs is the same water that your brain needs. The oil that you put into your car can be equated with the essential fatty acids that you need to put into your brain. Essential fatty acids (EFAs) are simply Omega oils, especially Omega 3 and 6. The petrol that your brain needs is the low-GI carbohydrates (don't worry, we will explain this later). Proteins are also very important, as they promote growth and maintenance of both the body and the brain. They are, therefore, the thing that maintains our brain's 'bodywork'. If you look after your child's brain in the same way that you maintain your car, you won't go wrong nutritionally. Ultimately, it can mean the difference between your child's brain performing like a battered old Beetle, or a sleek and sporty BMW.

Water

About 70 per cent of the body is made up of water. Proper hydration is vitally important for the smooth running of the body's systems and, of course, for the brain. Water helps you in a number of different ways. It transports nutrients throughout your body. It helps to deliver oxygen to all the cells. It removes waste products. It binds free radicals. It helps you to regulate your temperature and allows your body to repair, restore and heal itself. It is, in fact, essential for our well-being, yet most people do not drink enough water. We also tend to excrete, through urinating and perspiring, more water than we take in, and we also exhale water in the form of water vapour every time we breathe out.

So, in the same way that you top up your car's water tank regularly, make sure that you top up your child's water regularly. This means encouraging your child to drink enough pure water every day. Children need to drink at least four glasses of water a day (i.e. one litre of pure water). Things such as milk, fruit juice, flavoured water, tea, coffee and other fizzy soft drinks, do not count as water. Rooibos and other herbal teas, though, are considered water sources, as they do not contain caffeine or added sugar – so your body can use them in the same way that it uses water.

It is particularly important for children to be able to sip water throughout the day, especially during class, as the brain needs to be hydrated to work efficiently. Many schools now allow children to have bottles of water to sip from during class. If this is not possible, then make sure that your child drinks some water at breakfast and some more during break.

Headaches, constipation and lethargy can often be signs of dehydration. Make sure that your child is drinking enough water, and these should disappear. A good guideline to see whether your child is drinking enough water is to check the colour and odour of their urine. It should be light yellow and have hardly any smell. If it is dark yellow and does have a strong smell, your child is not drinking enough water.

While the importance of water is indisputable, getting your car to 'drink' water can be a lot easier than getting your child to drink it. Unfortunately, drinking pure water can be a bit like doing homework – not the most interesting option available. Here are some tips for developing a water-friendly child:

- **LIMIT CHOICES**
Avoid having many other drink choices in your home. If you offer your child water and there is a fizzy drink in the fridge, you are setting up a scenario for an argument. What also works well is to offer only two choices.

Would you like apple juice or water?

Amazingly, many children choose water (they will, if we don't 'teach' them to have a sweet tooth). If they choose apple juice, then water it down. You can start by pouring half juice, half water, and then – over time – decreasing the amount of juice that you put in the cup. You want to end up with your child drinking water with just a hint of juice or with no juice at all.

- **MODEL HEALTHY HABITS**

It is no good telling your child to drink water if he or she sees you sipping a cup of coffee or a cola. The best way to encourage your child to drink water is by doing so yourself.

- **TAKE SMALL SIPS**

Drinking four glasses of water can feel a little like eating the proverbial elephant. Try not to fill a large jug of water, which your child must finish by the end of the day. Unless your child is an avid water-drinker, seeing that large amount of water may be overwhelming. Rather portion out the water into small glasses (125 ml at a time) throughout the day. These little portions can be finished in a few swallows.

- **WATER BOTTLES AND STRAWS**

Using 'fun' water bottles and fancy straws can encourage your child to drink water. Children will almost always prefer to drink water from a bottle or through a straw than from a plain cup or glass.

- **OTHER FUN IDEAS**

Freeze water in ice-lolly moulds, or offer your child ice blocks in a bowl. Many children love to eat ice. You can also dilute fruit juice and freeze it. Give this to your child instead of store-bought ice-cream. Another good idea is to serve your child water with lots of crushed ice. You could also offer them sparkling water. Some children love the bubbles.

Handy hints

✍ Juice should never be used to quench a thirst. Always give your children water when they are thirsty. They can then be given small amounts of sweeter juice once their thirst has been quenched.

✍ Make it a rule that if your child wants a drink with a meal you only give them water.

✍ Always take a bottle of water in the car when you go on trips or outings. Children are bound to get thirsty, and then they ask you to buy them a cool drink.

Oil

What happens to your car when it runs out of oil? The moving parts seize up, and you land up with a massive bill. Oil lubricates the moving parts and makes sure that the whole system can move easily and smoothly without jerking, sticking or straining. In the same way, the oils that you put into your body help with the efficient functioning of your brain. Omega 3 and 6 fatty acids are particularly important, as they are essential for proper brain development and functioning. They also help to boost the body's immune system, hence their name 'Essential Fatty Acids' (EFAs).

Today's typical diet often consists of too much Omega 6 fat and too little Omega 3. It therefore becomes important that you focus on getting more Omega 3 into your child's diet. Omega 3 is found in things such as pilchards, sardines, salmon, mackerel, herring, anchovies, Omega 3-rich eggs, flax oil (linseed), canola oil and walnuts. There are also a number of good supplements on the market that can boost your child's Omega 3 intake, but try not to give them supplements to the exclusion of eating the foods that contain Omega 3. Omega 3-rich fish should be included at least twice a week in your family diet to ensure healthy brain functioning and to help your family cope with potential allergies.

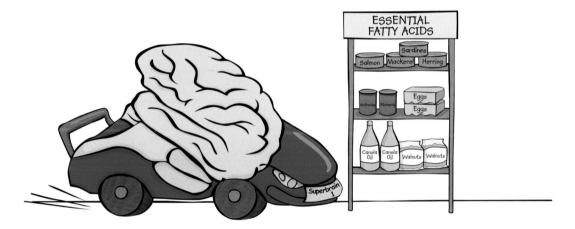

It is also not as simple as just boosting your child's Omega 3 intake. You also have to watch their trans-fatty acids intake. Trans-fatty acids raise blood cholesterol levels and increase one's risk of developing heart disease. They can also affect brain functioning, because they interfere with the role of Omega 3 fatty acids in the brain. Trans-fatty acids are found in brick margarines, shortening, commercial frying fats and high-fat baked goods such as pies and doughnuts. They are produced in the hydrogenation process which is widely used in the food industry to harden unsaturated oils. Any product that contains hydrogenated fat or hardened vegetable oil as an ingredient contains trans-fats, so read food labels and avoid these at all costs.

Proteins

As we've already mentioned, protein is essential for growth and maintenance of the body and brain. According to dieticians Steenkamp, Merlin and Wellmann (2006), children need more protein than adults in relation to their body weight. This does not mean that children must eat a bigger portion of meat, fish or chicken than an adult, but that they must have protein at every meal. Instead of eating three big meals a day, it is better for children (for all of us, in fact) to eat four to five small meals a day. For children, each of these meals must include a protein. The portion of protein that your child needs to eat is the size of their hand.

Protein is a complex food, and it takes the body a while to break it down. While it is being broken down, it continually gives you energy. The brain needs this energy to function efficiently; to think and reason, plan and organise and to pay attention and concentrate.

Meat, chicken, eggs and fish are rich sources of protein. If you buy Omega 3-rich eggs and fish such as pilchards, sardines, salmon, herring and mackerel, you will be giving your child a good source of protein as well as increasing their Omega 3 intake.

Always give your child proteins that are lean (lower in fat). Buy lean cuts of meat and remove all the visible fat and skin before cooking. Processed meat, such as sausages, viennas, chicken nuggets and salami, is high in fat and therefore not a good source of protein. These should not be eaten too often.

Proteins can also be obtained by eating dairy products such as yoghurt and lower-fat cheeses. These are good choices for children, as they supply them with other important vitamins and nutrients. However, always remember to choose the lower-fat options, or these items can be fattening. Nuts are also good, but can be very fattening, so only give your child a handful at a time.

Legumes are one of the best sources of protein. Legumes are things such as lentils, beans (baked beans, white beans, butter beans, etc); soya and chick peas. Not only do they provide the body with protein, but they are absorbed slowly by the body, which means that they keep you fuller and provide energy for longer. Legumes are very nutritious, and they add lots of fibre to a meal as well as lowering the fat content of the meal. They really can be the magic ingredient in your cooking, so try and hide them in as many meals as possible, even if you have to liquidise them!

Low GI Foods

All foods affect your blood glucose levels. Carbohydrates have a direct effect on your blood glucose levels, while the effect of proteins and fats is more indirect. It is important to know the effect that a particular food will have on your blood glucose levels, as you want to keep these levels within the normal range so that your body and brain can function optimally. The brain, in particular, is very sensitive to changes in blood glucose levels.

When digested, all foods containing carbohydrates are broken down into the simplest sugar, called glucose. Glucose is the fuel that gives the body and brain energy to function, meaning carbohydrates are your primary source of 'petrol'.

Many different foods contain carbohydrates. These include starches, cereals, legumes, breads and other products made of flour; sugar, sweets, vegetables, fruits and dairy products. But not all carbohydrates affect our blood glucose levels in the same way. They are made up of different lengths of chains of various types of sugars packed tightly or loosely together. Because of this, some are easier to break down into glucose, resulting in a faster release of the glucose into the bloodstream. Carbohydrates are, therefore, categorised according to the effect that they have on blood glucose levels.

Carbohydrates are classified as high-GI, low-GI or intermediate-GI. 'GI' is the Glycaemic Index. The Glycaemic Index is a measure, on a scale of 1 to 100, of how fast or slow a carbohydrate-containing food is digested and absorbed (Steenkamp, Merlin & Wellmann, 2006). It gives an indication of the rate at which carbohydrates affect the blood glucose levels after being eaten. High-GI foods result in a steep rise and a rapid fall in blood glucose levels. Lower-GI foods result in a slow and steady release of glucose. These are, therefore, far better to eat. If you wish to find out more about the Glycaemic Index and want to know the exact GI value of particular foods, you can speak to your local dietician or visit the website of the Glycaemic Index Foundation of South Africa (GIFSA) at www.gifoundation.com.

Here is a list of some low-GI foods that children usually like, taken from the *Shortened Glycaemic Index List of South African Foods* (Steenkamp, Merlin & Wellmann, 2006):

- Low-fat or fat-free milk (plain and flavoured).
- Milo.
- Low-fat and fat-free yoghurts.
- Low-fat or fat-free custard.
- ProNutro Original and ProNutro whole-wheat (Original and Apple Bake).
- Cooled mealie meal.
- Oats-so-easy (Natural).
- Provita.
- Pasta made from durum wheat or durum semolina.
- Baked beans.
- Tastic white and brown rice.
- Corn-on-the-cob or sweetcorn.
- Sweet potato.
- Deciduous fruit and berries (e.g. pears, peaches, plums, apples, strawberries and cherries).
- Citrus fruit (e.g. oranges, naartjies, grapefruit and lemons).
- Canned fruit (all of the above in fruit juice).
- Most cooked and raw vegetables (you will need to check the GI list to make sure).
- Homemade popcorn.
- Instant pudding made with low-fat milk.
- Drinks such as Sustagen and Ensure.

There are quite a few yummy foods on this list, so make sure that you choose wisely and give your child the best quality 'petrol'. Things such as sweets, biscuits, cakes, muffins, white and brown bread, energy drinks and sugary cereals are all high-GI, and will 'spike' your child's blood sugar levels and then drop them quickly after that. This will leave your child feeling tired, grumpy and lethargic. A tired, grumpy, lethargic child is not a happy child!

Optimal eating throughout the day

Remember that children have little tummies, so they do not need to eat big portions. In fact, forcing little children to finish three big meals a day may set them up to become weighty overeaters.

It is a lot easier for children to get all their nutrition through five small meals spaced evenly through the day. This would be breakfast; a mid-morning snack at school; lunch; a mid-afternoon snack and supper. Remember that children need to eat balanced meals, and that each meal must contain a protein.

Brain-booster breakfasts

Breakfast is essential. While your child may think he or she can go for long periods without eating, your child's brain disagrees. The brain cannot go from supper the previous evening to school break or even lunch without sustenance. Its water, protein and EFA levels will start to drop and your child will feel hungry, tired, irritable and, worst of all, will not be able to concentrate optimally in class.

Breakfast is not always an easy time to get children to eat. Some children are robust morning eaters, and others cannot even look at an egg, let alone eat one. Poor morning eating can be made worse by a hectic, stressful morning rush where there is little time to eat and where everything has to be gulped down.

To help poor morning eaters, keep meals small, quick and easy to eat. Try to keep breakfasts nutritionally rich, as opposed to merely big. A piece of cheese on half (or even a third) of a slice of multi-grain toast with a few slivers of apple or banana and a small glass of homemade orange-flavoured water is a far better nutritional option than a big bowl of sugar-frosted cereal with full-fat milk. Scrambled egg on toast or peanut butter on toast are two other good options. Otherwise, try a bowl of oats porridge or ProNutro, but only the Original or Apple Bake flavours.

Another breakfast option is to whiz up a smoothie. A small glass of a highly nutritious smoothie is easy to consume and will keep your child going until mid-morning break, when they can face something more solid.

Here is one good idea for a smoothie:

PEANUT BUTTER BRAIN BOOSTER
- 2 peeled, sliced bananas (low-GI).
- Small tub yoghurt (preferably plain).
- 25ml peanut butter (protein and EFA).
- A spoon of malt (optional EFA).
- Honey to taste.

Whiz these ingredients together. Add some water to thin if necessary.

You can throw any combination of fruit and yoghurt together to make delicious smoothies. Top these up with milk, to thin if necessary. Your child may even love you for making milkshakes for breakfast!

If all else fails, try a protein drink such as Sustagen or Ensure.

Sustaining school break snacks

Keep tuck money and treats to a minimum. They are part of your child's reward system, and should be earned.

Make sure that school lunch has some protein and/or a low-GI food to sustain your child's energy and concentration for the rest of the school day.

Always pack water in a refillable water bottle. Try to avoid energy drinks and all fizzy drinks. These are not good for children, and are not really thirst-quenching, because they are so sweet. They can send your child into a sugar 'overdrive', making it very hard for them to focus, and often with a negative effect on their behaviour.

Remember, this is a snack that will be eaten in about five to ten minutes; not a picnic. You do not need to pack a hamper of delicacies.

The rest of the day

Your lunch, afternoon snack and supper continue along the same lines. Keep the meals small and highly nutritious by including a protein and/or low-GI food and something containing an EFA. Don't forget the water. The afternoon protein or low-GI snack may be the best thing that you ever introduce into your home, as this often helps to prevent 'suicide hour' between 5 and 7pm when everybody's blood sugar levels have dropped and they are tired and irritable!

So, when you are next in the supermarket and staring at the vast array of foods, food supplements, vitamins and beverages, just keep thinking 'water, oil and petrol; water, oil and petrol', and you won't go wrong.

Handy hints

✎ If your child is battling to finish a meal, encourage them to finish the protein or low-GI food first.

✎ It is unnecessary to ban all 'junk' foods. There are few things as miserable as a child who is not allowed to eat sweets and cake at a birthday party. Just keep these to a minimum.

✎ The ability to understand nutrition and make healthy food choices is a life skill. Passing this skill on to your child is a wonderful gift, because it means lifelong health and vitality.

---

12 Discipline

My kids never stop fighting!

My child whines and whines. It drives me mad!

I send him to his room, but it doesn't seem to help!

My child told me that he hates me because I'm always shouting!

As soon as I'm on the phone, he needs me. I can't get a moment to myself!

I feel that all I ever do is punish my kids. I'm such a witch!

To teach, to learn, to grow

Many behavioural problems in the home are really the result of poor planning and organisation. When children do not have a plan of action to follow or firm, well-communicated boundaries, they feel confused and out of control. They behave in a confused and out-of-control manner. As most of this book has been about establishing rules and routines in a fair and positive way, at least some difficulties – particularly those involving tidying up, the morning and evening routine, and homework – should have been ironed out by now.

If, however, you are still struggling with inappropriate behaviour, you need to look a bit more deeply into the concept of discipline to try and understand what may be driving your child to be difficult. This way you'll be better equipped to deal with the behaviour.

Remember, if you think that understanding and dealing with your child's behaviour is difficult, it is just as difficult and confusing for them. This quote from an unknown author sums it up beautifully:

'We spend the first two years of our children's lives teaching them to walk and talk. We then spend the next 16 years teaching them to sit down and shut up!'

This can only be confusing!

What is discipline?

To 'discipline' means to teach. Discipline is, therefore, an intervention designed to teach a new behaviour or way of thinking. When you discipline your child, you need to intervene when he or she behaves inappropriately. But it is important that your intervention does not just stop the inappropriate behaviour. It must also teach a new appropriate form of behaviour or way of thinking. When true discipline structures are in place, children really do learn from their mistakes.

To 'punish', on the other hand, means to penalise – to cause pain, loss, or suffering. It also usually involves being treated in a harsh manner. When you punish a child, you often slap some arbitrary consequence onto the behaviour in the hope that it will stop very quickly and never be repeated. Punishment usually does stop inappropriate behaviour, but it can also cause a whole lot of underlying problems, of which we are often unaware. This will be discussed in more detail later in the chapter. Also, no useful learning comes out of punishment. Children learn what not to do, but are not helped to understand why their behaviour is inappropriate or taught alternatives to that behaviour. This is why children who are punished often become repeat offenders. They have an underlying need that must be met, but they do not know what else to do in order to try and meet this need in a more acceptable way.

All children (all people, in fact, no matter how young or old) behave in certain ways to meet certain needs. When people behave in a favourable manner, they are usually met with a favourable response. When they behave in an inappropriate manner, they often end up in some sort of trouble. When your child behaves inappropriately, it usually makes you angry. Anger blocks one's ability to think clearly and rationally. So, in anger, you react to your child's bad behaviour and often say or do something that you regret. In anger, parents have said to their children, 'I hate you' or 'I wish you had never been born.' It is very difficult to take these words back, and they often have significant, long-term effects on a child. In anger, parents also punish themselves. They say things like, 'No television for three weeks,' and after two days all they want to do is plonk their child down in front of the TV for a short while so that they can have a break. Or they say, 'We are not going to Granny's house this afternoon,' and then they find themselves stuck at home with children behaving in a very bratty manner – when in fact it is the parents who needed the break and to go to Granny's even more than the children. When parents are angry, they also often say things that they cannot carry out, and this makes their discipline very ineffective. For example, they say, 'If you don't stop doing that, you will not go to Michael's party,' when it fact they have already replied to the invitation and bought the gift. They also know that it is bad manners not to arrive at a party if you have said that you will be attending, so of course their child is going to the party. Because they cannot carry out what they have said, their child quickly learns that they don't mean what they say and continues to behave in an inappropriate way.

When disciplining your child it is important to try and separate the motive of the behaviour from the action. All behaviour has a purpose or need, and this need is very seldom bad. It is merely the way that the child goes about trying to meet the need that may not always be acceptable. Your job as a parent is to help your child find the need that underlies his or her behaviour, and then teach him or her a more appropriate way to meet the need. We also need to remember to do this with kindness, firmness, dignity and respect. Is this not the way that you would like to be treated if you did something wrong? Well, children have the same needs as adults, and they too would like to be treated in this way.

What drives human behaviour?

It is easy to say that you have to help your child understand the need that is driving his or her behaviour. However, you are not a mind-reader, so how do you do this? In simple terms, all humans (again, no matter how young or old) have two basic needs that drive all behaviour; a need to belong, and a need for independence or autonomy. While these two concepts might seem contradictory, or self-cancelling, in reality they are not.

The need to belong

Humans are social beings, and have a powerful need to belong to a group.

You want to feel that if you disappeared off the face of the earth, someone would notice that you were missing and someone would miss you. If you have a sense of belonging, you feel emotionally safe and you have a sense of worth; that your very existence matters. It is this need that often drives sibling rivalry. While you are engaging with one child, your other child feels like he or she doesn't belong and so does something (usually inappropriate) to get your attention. Once you start to talk to them, even if it is to shout at them, they feel as though they belong once again. This need to belong is also important to consider when choosing a school for your child. There is no such thing as one 'best' school. The way you should choose a school for your child is to go and walk around the school, and get a feeling for the 'vibe' of the school. If you feel comfortable there and the people around you feel like your kind of people, there is a good chance that your child will be happy there. A child who feels like he or she belongs in a place often performs better in that environment. Being rejected, feeling as though you are not noticed or feeling that others are better than you is emotionally painful. When you feel hurt, you usually behave inappropriately.

The need for independence or autonomy

While we like to feel that we belong and that we have a safe emotional harbour in which to anchor, we also strive for autonomy or independence. Having a sense of independence means that you feel that you are a capable human being and that you have something worthwhile to contribute. Often, children with learning difficulties do not feel as though they are capable human beings, and this sometimes has a significant impact on their behaviour. Children who do well at school get constant praise and recognition and, therefore, have no need to misbehave. They have a strong sense of autonomy.

The need to belong and the need for independence or autonomy are very strong. If they are met, children have no need to act out. They usually also have a strong sense of self-esteem. If these needs are not being met, children may behave in an inappropriate manner and may also not feel good about themselves. It is important to note that discipline is not a simple matter, whereby you are trying to meet both of these needs in your child. You may be a parent who has provided a home in which your child feels that he or she belongs and is important, but your child may not feel like they belong in another environment, such as at school or in their circle of friends. This may then lead to inappropriate behaviour. You may also be fantastic at building your child's sense of independence and self-worth at home, but if they are not getting any recognition from their teachers or peers, they may not feel like capable, worthwhile individuals – and this will have a negative effect on their behaviour. This recognition from people outside the family becomes more and more important to children as they get older. They often don't believe you when you say that they are wonderful, fantastic, capable human beings, because you are their parents, and so you have to say these things. Also, parents can often be a little over-gushy and their compliments are not always sincere, so children stop believing them and need to get recognition from elsewhere in order to build their self-esteem.

It is also important to note that, as an adult, you have exactly the same needs driving your behaviour – and that sometimes your need clashes with that of your child. This usually causes problems. For example: you are going out to the shopping centre, and so have told your child to quickly get dressed. When your child comes out of the room, he or she looks like something the cat brought in. None of their clothes match, and perhaps his or her shoes are on the wrong feet. Instead of saying to your child something like, 'Wow – you managed to dress yourself, and you even remembered your shoes,' which would build your child's sense of independence, you say, 'Those clothes don't match. Come on, let me dress you – and you must put your shoes on the right feet.' In this way, you squash your child's sense of independence. You do this because you are going out 'on show', and you need to belong to the group of good, model, upstanding families. These families do not have children who are dressed badly! As a parent, what is required of you is that you put your needs aside in order to accommodate your child's needs. What you have to say to yourself is, 'I am a good parent, and good parents encourage children to dress themselves and acknowledge their efforts, so it does not matter what my child looks like; at least he or she tried to dress him or herself.'

> Look, dad! I dressed myself for the party. I'm ready to go!

> I am so proud of you for getting dressed all by yourself.

How do you meet your child's need for a sense of belonging?

Many parents say, 'But I tell my child that I love them and that they are special all the time.' This does not make children feel like they belong. It is easy to say, 'I love you.' You do not even have to look up from your computer screen or the newspaper to say it. Words do not always convey meaning. Sometimes we say 'I love you' too often, and so it loses its impact.

In order to build your child's sense of belonging, you have to love him or her unconditionally. Not because they made the 'A' team or because they got good marks at school, but simply because you gave birth to them and they are yours. You need to honour them, cherish them and value them regardless of their behaviour, skills or talents. Someone said that all children need from us as parents is for our eyes to light up whenever they walk into the room. For this to happen, you actually have to look up from what you are doing and notice them!

Spending time with your child also helps to build a sense of belonging. This doesn't mean going to watch them playing sport or do ballet, and then sitting and chatting to your own friends or talking on your cell phone. You actually have to watch them, and then comment afterwards on what you saw, so that they know that you were watching. It also means sometimes ignoring your phone and saying that the other person can wait while you are talking to or playing with your child. How often are children the ones who have to wait? If you do not run to answer the phone your child thinks, 'Wow, I am important! Mom or Dad wants to spend time with me.'

How do you meet your child's need for a sense of independence?

Make sure that you take note of the things your child can do, rather than just focusing on the things that he or she can't do. Point out their competencies. Sometimes children are not aware of these. Stay focused on the positives. We seldom notice the things that our children get right, let alone thank them, and equally seldom reward them for doing them. We are, however, too quick to notice the negative and to scream and shout and punish our children for doing these things. Catch your child being good. This means noticing and commenting on the things they do right at home. For example, whenever they remember to hang up their bath towel, put their clothes in the wash basket or take their lunchbox to the kitchen. This is much easier said than done, but if you focus on and notice positive behaviour, you will be surprised how often it is repeated. If children do not feel that their efforts are being noticed, they often stop trying.

Another way to build independence is to help your child when he or she is struggling with something. But be careful to only offer your help if it is necessary, and not to become over involved and do everything for your child. Work out where they are stuck, and then help them with the next step. In this way they may be able to carry on and finish what they were doing on their own. This then leads to a sense of satisfaction. If you jump in and do everything for your child in an effort to make their life easier, they may never develop a sense of independence.

It is also important to give your child some responsibilities in order to develop their sense of independence. How can a child learn to be responsible if he or she is never given any responsibilities? These responsibilities must, however, be manageable – such as feeding the dog, helping to set the table or tidying the bathroom after bath time. Children also need to be held accountable when these responsibilities are not carried out. If children are given the opportunity to help, they feel as though they are capable human beings with something worthwhile to contribute, whether at home or in the school environment.

What happens when these needs are not met?

If the need to belong or the need to be autonomous is not satisfied, a deep, subconscious craving can set in, which has a powerful influence on a child's behaviour. The child then behaves in a way that he or she thinks will help to meet these needs, but the behaviour is often inappropriate and causes them more trouble than good. What is most commonly seen is attention-seeking behaviour or power-struggles.

Attention seeking behaviour

'I ONLY BELONG WHEN I HAVE YOUR ATTENTION'

Mommy, mommy, mommy ...!

Children who constantly nag and whine for your attention are telling you, in the only way they know how, that they do not feel like they are important or that they belong. They are calling desperately for your attention – even if it is negative – in order to try and enhance their sense of belonging. It is important to note that children love positive attention (praise and encouragement). In fact, they can never get enough of it. If a child cannot get any positive attention, then he or she will try to get negative attention. Negative attention is better than no attention at all because if you don't get any attention, you don't feel as though you belong.

Parents have to be careful, because they often perpetuate attention-seeking behaviour without knowing it. How often do you come home to find your children playing nicely together? (Granted, this may not happen too often. More often than not, there are fights going on.) But if the children are playing nicely, we usually tip-toe past them and go and do something for ourselves. However, as soon as they start to fight, we drop everything and come running. In this way we give them negative attention.

It is OK to tip-toe past children when they are playing nicely. Often, if we disturb them, we spoil their game. However, later on in the day, you need to comment on their good behaviour and, even better, reward it. Say to your children something like, 'When I came home today, you were playing so nicely together, and I was able to get lots done. So tonight you guys can stay up 15 minutes later and we can play a game together.' In this way you are giving your children positive attention. Do this often, so that they learn that you do notice their good behaviour and that it pays to be good in your house. In this way, when your children start to fight, one may say, 'Hey, let's try and be good today in case mom or dad are watching. Maybe they will give us something nice.' Remember when, in Chapter 1, we discussed instant rewards, delayed gratification and intermittent rewards? These are very good for maintaining positive behaviour.

So remember to try and catch your children being good, and to let them know that you have noticed them. Try to ignore negative or attention-seeking behaviour as much as possible, unless of course it is dangerous and someone is going to get hurt. If you give this behaviour attention, your child will continue to nag, whine, moan or shout when you are around. If your child speaks to you inappropriately, tell him or her that your ears do not work when he or she talks like that, and then ignore them. The trick, however, is not to ignore your child for too long. Listen to them and, as soon as they start to talk nicely, answer back. In this way, your child learns that when he or she talks nicely, you respond. When he or she talks rudely or disrespectfully, you do not listen. Be very consistent about this, and you will have far less nagging, whining, moaning or shouting in your house.

Remember, the attention that children crave is to be counted, to be valued and to be acknowledged. Attention means really listening to your child and making eye contact when you have a conversation. Attention also means doing special things together. This builds a sense of belonging. Attention does not mean buying all the latest toys and gadgets. This is far easier, but only temporarily makes the child feel special, and then they need you to buy them something else.

Power struggles

'I BELONG ONLY WHEN I'M WINNING OR IN CHARGE, OR AT LEAST WHEN I DON'T LET *YOU* WIN'

This type of scenario has little to do with getting dressed, and everything to do with the start of autonomy and independence. It is also the result of a clash of needs. The daughter needs to become independent and make her own choices, and the mom needs to feel that she belongs to the group of 'good moms' who can get their children to school on time, clean, fed and well dressed. The two needs are striving to be met at the same time, which results in a fight.

Children love power struggles, because during a power struggle they have your full attention, and nobody else (i.e. other siblings) can have it. Also, while you are locked in a power struggle, they are usually managing to avoid the thing that you want them to do. Power struggles often occur over things such as homework, bathing, eating, tidying up and going to bed! Children will never be the first one to end a power struggle, because they get too much out of it. You, therefore, have to be the adult in the situation and walk away. Remember, the best way to end a power struggle is the offer the 'either ... or ...' option. This was discussed in detail in Chapter 3 of this book. 'Either you go and bath now, like I am asking you to, or you will go to bed early.' Remember that the 'or' must be something horrible in order to try and get your child to make the right choice. If they still do not do what you asked, you must make sure that you carry out the 'or', otherwise this will not prove to be an effective discipline technique for you.

Un-met needs can sometimes also result in revenge- or withdrawal-type behaviour. This kind of behaviour is often serious, and may require further intervention.

Revenge

'IT HURTS THAT I DON'T BELONG, BUT AT LEAST I CAN HURT BACK'

By the time children turn vengeful, they are telling you that they are emotionally damaged and hurting badly. They have tried attention-seeking behaviour and power struggles with no success in an effort to belong, so they begin to act out their hurt and pain. Vengeful feelings can fester for years. Children will often plot and plan and wait until they have the power to take revenge. This revenge can result in aggression and physically hurting people (You hurt me, so I will hurt you); delinquent behaviour such as stealing (You 'stole' from me, so I will steal from you); eating disorders (You 'starved' me of love and attention, so I will starve you of peace of mind) and drug abuse (You 'damaged' me, so I will damage your peace of mind). Remember, people who have been hurt, hurt other people.

This type of revenge is not the same as the revenge between siblings or friends. Children often work on the premise 'You broke something of mine, so I will break something of yours', or 'You hit me, so I will hit you'. This is not like the 'damaged' behaviour discussed above. It is, in fact, quite common behaviour. However, it is important that we intervene every time we see this behaviour and that we teach children that it is wrong. Both children in a revenge situation need to get into trouble in order to learn that revenge does not pay.

Withdrawal

'I GIVE UP – IT IS IMPOSSIBLE TO BELONG'

If children are attention-seeking, engaging in power struggles or even taking revenge, they are still fighting like mad to survive emotionally, even if they are going about it in the most misdirected and inappropriate way.

When children withdraw, they have given up because they realise that, no matter what they do, they will never belong, so why bother even trying? Children who withdraw do not socialise, are unresponsive, make no eye contact, and their body language is curled inwards and hunched over, which warns people not to intrude.

Children who withdraw are usually quite seriously emotionally damaged and have lost any sense of personal worth. They have come to learn that they are not worth fighting for and they lose their drive to survive on an emotional level. These children are highly vulnerable to activities such as joining gangs, which offer a great sense of belonging and family, to drug and alcohol abuse as a means to escape, and even to suicide, which is the ultimate withdrawal behaviour.

Think before you shout

If your child is misbehaving, it is really important to try and understand what is driving that behaviour. There are very, very few individuals who enjoy behaving inappropriately. All humans need to belong and to feel valuable and capable. Without someone to guide us, however, we sometimes get a bit confused about how we should act to meet these needs.

I understand WHY my kids fight, but WHAT MUST I DO?

What NOT to do

PUNISH

In the heat of the moment, it is very tempting to lash out and punish your child. Be careful though – punishment such as a good, hard smack 'works' in the short term; but often has negative long-term effects.

No child ever says 'thank you' to their parents for treating them harshly and humiliating them (usually in public). No; in fact they often feel very resentful towards their parents. What they feel is that life is unfair. Their parents have all the power, and they have none. They wait until they step into a position of power, and then wield this – over others, usually their own children later in life. They will hear themselves saying, 'You *will* do it, because I said so!', and unconsciously they are thinking 'because I am finally in charge!'

Punishment can also lead to revenge, as we've already discussed. Children who are treated harshly often think to themselves, 'They are winning now, but I will get even later.' This happens when a 16-year-old son turns around and hits his father back, and then that is the last hiding he ever gets. Another form of revenge is the child who stays at home and milks their parents for everything they have got. They let them pay for their school fees and tertiary education and then, the day that they get a job, they leave home and tell their parents that they will never see them again and that they will never get to see their grandchildren. An extreme form of revenge is when we hear of a child who returns to the family home later in life and murders his or her parents. We are all horrified when we hear something like this, but we have to ask ourselves, 'What did those parents do to their child to make him or her want to kill them?'

Punishment can also make someone rebellious. Remember that when someone is punished, they just have some arbitrary consequence slapped onto their behaviour – but they are not being helped to meet their underlying need. In this case what the child says is, 'You thought *that* was bad – just wait until you see what I come up with next!' This child spins out of control, because no one ever takes the time to find out why he or she is misbehaving.

Now you might be thinking, 'OK, but I was punished and I am not resentful. I was also not a rebel, and I definitely don't want to take revenge on my parents. In fact, they make quite good babysitters. So how can punishment be so bad?' Punishment not only leads to resentment, rebelliousness or revenge, but it can also lead to sneakiness. As we've already said, no one says 'thank you' to their parents for punishing them, and then never misbehaves again. What children learn from punishment is that if you get caught you will be in trouble again – and trouble is not much fun; so don't get caught. They then become devious and sneaky, and often rope in other people to keep watch while they carry on doing their naughty things. We also carry this through into adult life, and often tell 'white lies' to cover up when we do something bad, as we are so scared of being caught out because we anticipate a terrible consequence. We just can't seem to leave behind that childhood fear of getting into trouble.

Far worse than all of the above is the fact that punishment can damage self-esteem. Many people are raised believing that adults know best; and that adults are always right. Therefore, if an adult tells you that you are 'lazy', 'naughty', 'stupid' or 'useless', then you must be those things. This then becomes a self-fulfilling prophecy, and you grow up into an adult with low self-esteem. You may quite possibly get through your day remembering to do so many things, like get the kids to school on time, hand in your business proposal, do the shopping, fetch the kids, cook supper, etc – and then forget to phone your friend for her birthday.

What you say to yourself then is, 'You see, I *am* useless. I can't remember anything!' You can't hold on to all the good things you did during the day – instead you use the same 'stick' to beat yourself with that your parents used when you were a child.

It is a crazy idea that, in order to make children behave better, we first have to make them feel worse. When we are humiliated or treated unfairly we definitely do not feel like co-operating or doing better! Our usual responses are to give up, cover up or become 'approval junkies', giving up part of ourselves to please others. The same goes for children.

Tactics you should avoid
Adapted from the work of Katherine C. Kersey

BEING TOO PERMISSIVE

Children from permissive homes where 'anything goes' often grow up to be irresponsible, manipulative and unpleasant. They tend to develop a sense of entitlement, and think and act as if the world owes them a living. Nobody wants to be around a child who is spoiled, demanding and disrespectful.

Children need leadership and defined rules and boundaries. If there is a lack of leadership from parents, your child will fill that vacuum by becoming the leader – and you'd better believe that a family controlled by a seven-year-old is no fun. Remember, you do not need to be your child's friend. Your job is to be the parent.

SMACKING

Not an option! Children who are smacked will often learn to cope with difficult situations by smacking or hitting. Children need to have role models who have self-control, who handle their anger in constructive ways, and who settle their problems with their heads and not their hands. Many parents have admitted to feeling out-of-control when they lash out verbally or physically at their children. This can lead to a vicious and painful attack, from which both parties struggle to recover. When people resolve to stop smacking, they are forced to look for other alternatives for discipline and often report liking themselves better as parents. Furthermore, studies have shown that children who are not hit are more likely to find non-physical ways to settle their differences with siblings and friends.

EMBARRASSMENT AND HUMILIATION

Nobody likes being embarrassed in front of people. Embarrassing or humiliating your child may get immediate results in that it stops the behaviour for the time being; but more often than not these techniques cause horrible damage to self-esteem and trust. Someone who has been embarrassed or humiliated usually responds by withdrawing or by retaliating (the power struggle and revenge cycle). If you try to control your child by embarrassing them, there is a strong chance he or she will start to dislike you, and you will lose their respect and trust. Embarrassment can also make your child feel as though they are a failure, and they can develop feelings of self-doubt or hatred as a result.

ORDERING

Ordering stifles a child's growing need for independence and autonomy. When you order your child around you may create conflict, dislike and the urge to rebel. Children who are routinely ordered around will retaliate by 'pushing their parents' buttons', because they are driven to satisfy the need for independence. Ordering frequently leads to power struggles, and no one really wins a power struggle without some pain and loss.

TAKING AWAY FAVOURED THINGS

Taking away things that children value, as a form of punishment, can lead to feelings of resentment and retaliation. If you feel the need to take away something of value, then do so for a short period of time. For example, 'You can't watch TV tonight,' rather than, 'You can't watch TV.' There is no way you can keep up this punishment indefinitely and, as soon as you give in, your youngster has won the battle and gains power leverage over you. You also need to be careful of stopping children's hobbies; such as sport, gymnastics, karate or dancing. Children often need these activities as a stress release. If you stop them, your child's behaviour may deteriorate even more.

NEGATIVE LABELLING

Labels, for example 'My little trouble-maker', 'Our little noise-maker' or 'Little Miss Fussy' have a way of becoming self-fulfilling prophecies. Children believe what they hear about themselves, and often have tremendous faith in adults and the perceptions that adults have. We should rather use labels to our advantage and say good things about children, so that they aim to live up to the good things being said about them. (But be careful of putting too much pressure on your child and trying to make him or her live up to things that they may not be capable of, for example, 'My little Einstein' or 'My perfect boy'.)

ARGUING

Getting into arguments with your child is non-productive and, as we've already mentioned, you may find yourself saying things that you regret, or that are hurtful to your child. Arguments are often quite beneficial to your child, as this way he or she gets your full attention. Arguing can maintain or even strengthen an inappropriate behaviour; especially if your child may be feeling in need of some attention. If we refuse to argue, there will be no argument – but the matter can still be discussed (possibly a bit later, when everyone has calmed down). Discussions are healthy, but arguing is counter-productive.

THOUGHTLESS THREATS

Adults often make ridiculous, impossible threats in the heat of the moment which they cannot enforce at all. Useless threats are more than useless for changing behaviour. Your child knows full well that you cannot follow through on your threats, so they shrug you off and again you lose credibility as a parent. If your child is driving you mad, catch hold of yourself by counting to ten (or 20 on a bad day!) before shouting, 'If you don't stop crying, I'll give you something to really cry about!'

PLEADING AND BEGGING

When you plead and beg with your children, they quickly realise that you are not in a leadership role. They then have the upper hand, and lose respect for you. Your children need you to be in control, to say what you mean and to back it up with action.

SCARING

Scare tactics often appear to work, as children obey immediately because they are frightened – but the long-term effects can be disastrous. Threats – especially those that threaten to remove a child from a family or from a school – not only scare children, but disrupt their sense of safety and belonging. Over time, children lose respect for those who manipulate them with scare tactics when they are young and vulnerable. A huge part of parenting is to make children feel emotionally and physically safe in a world that is full of scary things. Adding to the burden of external threats will exacerbate inappropriate behaviour in the long term. Not only does scaring not work as a form of discipline, but you stand a real chance of creating a highly anxious child who is scared of you and who obeys you out of fear, not respect.

LOSING YOUR COOL

Children need someone older and wiser to be in charge. When an adult is seen or thought to be no longer in control, children are frightened. They usually imitate the adult's behaviour and yell and go berserk as well. Nothing productive is gained through this kind of interaction.

BEING VAGUE

Children need you to be clear, concise and to the point. When you are vague, for example saying, 'Be good,' 'Straighten up' or 'Be quiet,' children don't really know what you mean. It is better to say to a child, 'Please stop rustling that paper' than 'Be quiet,' because if they are not talking, they may not understand what you mean.

LAUGHING AT MISBEHAVIOUR

Sometimes we confuse children by giving them mixed signals when they misbehave; such as laughing the first time a child misbehaves, but then becoming angry and punishing the child when the behaviour continues.

EXPECTING YOUR CHILD TO READ YOUR MIND

Although children are perceptive and quickly pick up on the emotional state of those around them, they cannot read your mind. They need to be told, very clearly, what is expected of them, especially in new situations.

The guilt kicks in ...

By now you may be feeling guilty, because there is a good chance that you probably make use of one or many of these 'discipline' techniques. Don't beat yourself up about it. We all make mistakes, and many of us discipline our children in the same way that we were disciplined by our parents and teachers. Most of us simply follow the patterns of behaviour that are familiar to us, and often do not use different techniques because we don't know any better.

The five steps to effective discipline

Adapted from the work of John F. Taylor Ph.D.

True discipline is a process of learning, for both you and your child. If punishment is the norm in your home, then introducing actual discipline will involve quite a change in thinking.

STEP 1: INTERVENE EARLY

As soon as you hear a squabble or trouble brewing, you need to try and interrupt the interaction as quickly as possible before the anger escalates. Do not stay seated and think to yourself, 'This is going to end in tears,' because when you have children who are angry or upset coming to look for you, you have a long process to go through to solve the problem. Rather get up and go to where the trouble is. Look your children in the eye and say something in a firm, no-nonsense voice like, 'Stop fighting now, or I will switch off the TV' or 'Stop fighting now, or I will take that toy away.' But you need to be serious about what you say. If you turn your back and the children continue fighting, then turn around and switch the TV off or take the toy away. There does not have to be any further consequence. Now that your children don't have something to fight over, they have to go off and find something else to do. You may have to do this a couple of times for them to learn that you are serious about what you say.

If you take something away from your children, such as a toy, don't let them have it back for the rest of the day. Once they are asleep you can put it back with the rest of the toys for them to play with again tomorrow. If they were not allowed to watch TV, tell them that they can try again tomorrow to see if they can watch TV nicely together. You should have a much more favourable outcome when they engage in the activity the next day.

If you manage to intervene in time by using your body language, a stern, steady voice and the 'either/or' strategy, the situation will often calm down quite quickly.

STEP 2: CREATE BREATHING SPACE (TIME OUT)

If you miss this first step and don't interrupt in time, everyone involved usually becomes very angry – which creates an emotional climate ripe for accusations, threats and smacks, and the situation usually ends in tears (with sometimes even the parents crying).

Instead of becoming involved and adding your anger to an already heated mix, rather separate your children. Send each child off to a different part of the house – for example: 'You go to your room, and you go to your room,' or 'You go to the front garden and you to the back garden,' or even 'You go to the TV room, and you go to the playroom.' You could even say to older children, 'I am going to the kitchen to make myself some tea to calm down. Where are you going, and where are you going?' Each child then gets to choose the place where they would like to go to calm down. Yes; this is not a punishment, but a time for tempers to cool off and for everyone to settle down so that they can think rationally. Remember what we said earlier – when people are angry they don't think rationally, and they usually do or say something they later regret.

Anger, in itself, is not a bad thing. We all feel angry from time to time. It is what you do with your anger that can be good or bad. Don't make your child feel bad about being angry; teach him or her that whenever they are angry they need to remove themselves from the situation to prevent themselves from doing or saying something that they will regret. It is an emotionally mature person who can recognise when they are feeling angry and call time out so that they can compose themselves and come back and deal with the situation in a rational manner. This is what you want to teach your child.

Angry feelings should not be submerged, where they can fester into revenge. Feelings have a physical element that needs to be released. This is why you bounce up and down when you are excited or scream and shout when you are angry or hurt. As a parent you need to teach your child healthy, appropriate ways of working through and reducing difficult feelings, so that they do not become pent-up and explode at inappropriate times. Children need to be encouraged to release or express their anger in ways that do not hurt people either physically or emotionally. This can be done though physical activities like shredding paper, punching a punch bag, squashing a stress ball or doing some physical exercise like running, riding a bike or swimming lengths of a pool. As the anger is released physically, rational thought returns. Some children find that listening to music or writing out their feelings helps to calm them down. Just removing some children from an angry situation and letting them play quietly on their own can help to calm them down. You need to experiment and see what works best for your child. The only rules with anger are that you may not hurt anyone (either by hitting, kicking, pinching, punching or biting, or with hurtful words), and you may not break anything. Make these a rule in your house for everyone to follow. But remember that when you do, you remove smacking from your repertoire, as you usually only hit your child when you are angry and can't think of anything else to do.

This cooling off period is not to be confused with the well-known, 'Go to your room and wait until your father gets home.' This form of punishment uses fear, and is not at all helpful. Separating children and giving them some breathing space is the best thing that you can do for an angry child. This gives everyone some time to calm down and gather their composure, including you.

STEP 3: ACKNOWLEDGE FEELINGS

Children sitting in their rooms are usually waiting for their parents to come and shout at them and tell them how naughty they are. This is pretty pointless, as they often know what they have done wrong. Also, we have discussed how shouting at children and punishing them does not teach them more appropriate behaviour.

When you go into your child's room, ask them why they are there. If they say that it is because they were naughty, tell them that this is not true. They are in their room merely to calm down. Then check that your child is calm. If they need more time, walk away and come back a bit later. If they are calm, you can sit down and have a private and honest conversation with your child. Sending your child to their room for a while and then letting them come out again and join the family without taking time to talk the problem through will not teach your child anything. This is why people say that 'time out' doesn't work. They use it as a punishment, instead of simply as a calming-down period.

When you do go in to talk to your child, the first thing that you need to do is to acknowledge his or her feelings. You do this by saying something like: 'All you want to do is be with your big brother, and he doesn't always want you around. That must be hard.' A little bit later you have a similar conversation with your other child in another room and say, 'All your little brother ever wants is to be with you. That must be very irritating at times.' In this way you create a win-win situation where both children feel that you understand their side of the story. If you deal with two angry children who are standing next to each other, you are always the loser. One of them will tell you that you are unfair, and that you always take sides. Also, by acknowledging your child's feelings you are not necessarily accepting their behaviour. All you are saying is that it is OK to feel the way they do, but at no stage do you say that their behaviour is acceptable. For example, 'It is OK to be irritated by your younger brother, but it is *not* OK to hit him.' If you are not sure how your child is feeling, simply use a universal empathy statement such as, 'This is a very hard time for you.' This also works well.

By going in and empathising with your child, you open the channels of communication. Your child feels that you understand him or her and is, therefore, more willing to work with you. If you go in and shout at your child then you close the channels of communication, because your child now has to protect him or herself from your verbal attack.

Empathy and the will to really get to the bottom of the situation can be the keys to true discipline. You can convey empathy quite easily by doing one of the following:

- Listening (e.g. 'Tell me more about how you feel').
- Understanding (e.g. 'I understand how you feel').
- Accepting (e.g. 'I accept that this is how you feel').
- Identifying (e.g. 'I would feel that way too').
- Caring (e.g. 'I wish you happiness and don't want you to have this painful feeling').
- Having a desire to help (e.g. 'How can I help you so that you will feel better?').

STEP 4: TEACH PROBLEM-SOLVING SKILLS

This is the part where the true discipline takes place. Remember, discipline means to teach – and what you want to teach is a more appropriate way of behaving.

The first thing you need to do is make sure that your child understands what they did wrong, and why it is wrong. Don't, during this stage, say things like, 'You make my heart sad when you behave like this,' or 'You make your brother cross when you tease him.' Children often struggle to put themselves in other people's shoes, and so all they think is 'So what?' You need to turn their behaviour around and ask them how they would feel if it happened to them. Then sit back and listen. Children can be very vocal in telling you how they would feel, and what they think should happen to the other person. After they are finished, tell them that this is how their brother (or the other injured partner) is feeling. This is to develop empathy in your child and to teach them to put themselves in other people's shoes.

Many parents get as far as this step, but you still haven't taught your child other, appropriate behaviour – so there is a good chance that they will go out and repeat the behaviour for which they have just been in trouble. In order to say that you have truly disciplined your child, you need to teach him or her problem-solving skills. You do this by asking them what they could do next time that they are in a similar situation. For example, if your one child had a toy, and the other one tried to grab it, and it is now broken, ask your child what he or she could do the next time someone has their toy. In the beginning, your child may struggle to come up with alternatives, and you may have to help them. But with time and practice, your child will become better and better at thinking up more appropriate solutions to his or her problems. We all have the capacity to do this. The problem is that when we are angry, the first thought that comes into our mind is an impulsive thought, and it usually gets us into trouble. If we take the time to stop and think, we can often come up with far better ideas. Many children, however, do not stop, think and then act. They act first, and then think and often end up saying, 'Oops,' because they know that what they have done is wrong.

If you spend time problem-solving with your child when he or she is calm and rational, you can pre-programme some good ideas into his or her head – and hopefully, the next time he or she is angry, these ideas will pop into their mind first.

When problem-solving with your child over the toy that got grabbed and broken, you could come up with the following ideas:

- Grab the toy again and it may or may not get broken (leave this option there, as it is the one that they have just chosen. You want them to decide whether or not it is an appropriate way of behaving).
- Come and ask for help (this is often the only alternative that we give children, but then we also say things like, 'When I am on the phone, don't interrupt me.' So if you are not around, or if you are on the phone, the only other choice that your child has is to go back and grab the toy!).
- Go and get another toy that you know the person likes, and try and swap them; or
- Pretend not to be interested in the toy, and when the person puts it down, go and get it and have a chance to play with it.

Once you have brainstormed these ideas, do not tell your child which one to choose. Say to him or her, 'Next time you are in a similar situation, choose one of these options and try it. If you land up back in this room having this same conversation with me, then cross out that behaviour and put it in the box of never-to-be-repeated behaviours. If it gets you a favourable outcome, remember it and try it again.'

Do not overwhelm your child with too many options, as this will just confuse him or her. Two or three options when they are younger, or three or four when they are older, are plenty.

This process may seem quite lengthy (that is why we recommended interrupting and intervening early); but it shouldn't take too long in reality. Do not sit in your child's room and have long conversations. They will get bored and tune out before you even get to the problem-solving section. You need to simply make sure that they understand what went wrong, why it is wrong, how the other person feels and what they can do next time. If a child knows all this, they will usually feel truly sorry for what they have done, and may even want to make amends. This is when you move on to the final step.

STEP 5: MAKE REPARATION AND REDIRECT

During this stage your child needs to make reparation for what he or she has done wrong. Sometimes a genuine apology will be enough, and then you can send your child off in a new direction to play with something else. However, sometimes there needs to be a further consequence to ensure that your child learns from his or her mistake. If a toy has been broken, for example, then your child may need to lose out on his or her pocket money this week in order to pay the other person for their loss. It is really difficult for a child to lose out on pocket money and to have to give it to a sibling. They then get nothing, and their sibling gets double. However, do not say to your child that they will not get pocket money again until they have paid for the toy. If the toy cost R300 and they only get R10 a week, it will take them 30 weeks to pay for the toy. By this time, nobody will even be able to remember what got broken! We can't always replace everything that we break or fix everything that we do wrong; but if we make some sort of effort, the person we have harmed will feel that justice has been served. With the little bit of extra money, your other child may be able to buy something else to play with.

Looking a little more closely at consequences

True discipline involves the concept of consequences. It is important for children to learn through the consequences of their actions. These consequences may be positive, or they may be negative. As a parent you should never rush in and try to protect your child from the consequences of his or her actions. The best way for a child to learn is through experiencing the natural consequence of an action.

A natural consequence is anything that happens naturally, without any adult interference. When you stand in the rain, you inevitably get wet. When you don't eat, you get hungry. When you don't learn for a test, you can expect a bad result.

No piggy-backing is allowed with natural consequences. A parent piggy-backs when he or she lectures, scolds, says, 'I told you so,' or does anything else that adds more blame, shame or pain than the child might experience naturally from the experience. Piggy-backing actually lessens the learning that can occur by experiencing a natural consequence, because your child stops processing the experience and focuses on absorbing or defending him or herself against the blame, shame and pain. Empathy, on the other hand, is allowed and is, in fact, encouraged, as it enhances the learning experience. For example, if your child does badly in a test because he or she did not prepare adequately, do not become angry or say, 'I told you so' (piggy-backing). Instead, just say something like, 'I'm sorry' (even if you don't mean it). Your child will now feel that they have let you down and this enhances the learning experience.

Using natural consequences would be the most obvious way of helping your child to learn the results of his or her behaviour. However, there are times when natural consequences are not practical, such as when a child is in danger (you cannot say, 'Don't run across the road,' and then stand back and watch your child learn from the natural consequence!), or when the natural consequences interfere with the rights of others (such as when your child is playing the fool in class and disturbing the other children) or when the results of your child's behaviour do not seem like a problem to him or her (such as when they fail a test because they did not learn, but are not at all concerned about their marks).

Under these circumstances it would be better to use logical consequences as a means of dealing with your child's behaviour. A logical consequence requires the intervention of an adult. You need to decide what kind of consequence would provide a helpful learning experience for your child. Logical consequences can be very effective when your child is involved in deciding what consequences would be most appropriate to help him or her learn.

In order to ensure that your logical consequence is, in fact, a logical consequence and not a punishment, you need to make sure that it is related to the behaviour. It does not help a child to say that they cannot play soccer today because they were naughty in Maths class. What have soccer and Maths got in common? If your child is naughty in Maths class, then he or she should get some extra Maths to complete – but if they are naughty on the sports field, then they must sit on the side and miss practice. If they are really naughty they must perhaps miss the next match, but just the next match, and not all the matches for the rest of the season. Logical consequences must also be reasonable. Your child must realise that he or she has done something wrong, must make reparation for their mistake, but must then be forgiven and given another chance. If you do not give your child another chance, how will he or she ever learn from his or her mistake?

Children can learn a great deal from both natural and logical consequences. However, when applying these concepts, make sure that you still treat your child with kindness, firmness, dignity and respect. Always take them aside and deal with their difficulties in a private manner. Remember that your child has the same basic needs that you have and would, therefore, like to be treated in the same way that you would like to be treated, especially when he or she has done something wrong. Children are human. They make mistakes, but if they are given the opportunity and assistance to learn from their mistakes they will turn out to be very well-adjusted adults and loving parents to your future grandchildren. What better gift can you give your child than true discipline?

Index

Italic entries: cartoons, **bold** entries: photographs

DEDICATION

We dedicate this book to all of the children who have passed through our lives,
challenged us, and made us learn.

From Jane Jarvis:
And especially to my two boys, C.J. and Peter Jarvis:
I am so grateful that you were entrusted into my care and I thank you for allowing me to
practice my parenting skills on you. I may not always have got it right, but please know that
everything I have ever done has been out of love for you.
And to my husband, Dave:
Thank you for teaching me that it is not only important to raise children
properly, but that it is also important to have fun whilst doing so!

From Debbie de Jong:
To Mike:
Thank you for endless cups of coffee, backrubs and much needed support.

BIBLIOGRAPHY

Clark, Lynn F., Ph.D.; Robb, J.: SOS Help for Parents – A Practical Guide forHandling Common Everyday Behaviour Problems (2nd edition). Parents' Pr, Kentucky (1996)

Dinkmeyer, Snr., Don; McKay, Gary D.; Dinkmeyer, James S.; Dinkmeyer, Jr., Don; McKay, Joyce L.: Parenting Young Children. Systematic Training for Effective Parenting of Children Under Six. American Guidance Service, Inc, Minnesota (1997)

Horsley, Kevin: A talk on 'How to Improve Memory', 27 August 2005, hosted by the Delta Park Remedial School, Johannesburg

Kersey, Katharine C., Ed.D.: Don't Take It Out On YourKids! A Parents' Guide to Positive Discipline (revised edition). Berkley Books, New York (1994)

Kohlberg, Lawrence: Essays On Moral Development, Vol 1, 'The Philosophy of Moral development'. Harper & Row (1981)

Nelsen, Jane, Ed.D.: Positive Discipline. Ballantine Books, New York (1996)

Steenkamp, Gabi; Merlin, Tanzia; Wellmann, Jeske: Sustained Energy for Kids. Tafelberg Publishers, Cape Town (2006)

Taylor, John F., Ph.D.: Helping Your ADD Child (revised 3rd edition). Prima Publishing, Roseville, California (2001)

Taylor, John F.: International Conference on 'Attention Deficit Hyperactivity Disorder and Other Co-morbid Disorders', 6—9 March 2002, Pretoria (various sessions)

Websites:

http://fitness.ygoy.com/health-effects-of-television/

http://kidshealth.org/parent/positive/family/tv_affects_child.html

http://news.webindia123.com/news/Articles/Health/20071210/845214.html

http://www.aoa.org/ (American Optometric Association)

http://www.babo.co.uk/vl.html (British Association of Behavioural Optometrists

http://www.earthlingcommunication.com/blog/teaching-your-child-listening-skills.php

http://www.library.nhs.uk/ChildHealth/

http://www.playattention.com/attention-deficit/articles/too-much-tv-lowers-tests-scores/

http://www.red-branch.com/

http://www.ynhh.org/pediatrics/index.html (Yale - New Haven Children's Hospital)